ON WRITING
(AND WRITERS)

ALSO BY C. S. LEWIS

Letters of C. S. Lewis

All My Road Before Me

The Business of Heaven: Daily Readings from C. S. Lewis

Present Concerns: Essays by C. S. Lewis

Spirits in Bondage: A Cycle of Lyrics

On Stories: And Other Essays of Literature

The Reading Life

A Preface to Paradise Lost

English Literature in the Sixteenth Century (Excluding Drama)

ALSO AVAILABLE FROM HARPERCOLLINS

The Chronicles of Narnia

The Magician's Nephew

The Lion, the Witch and the Wardrobe

The Horse and His Boy

Prince Caspian

The Voyage of the Dawn Treader

The Silver Chair

The Last Battle

C.S. Lewis

ON WRITING
(AND WRITERS)

A Miscellany of
Advice and Opinions

EDITED BY DAVID C. DOWNING

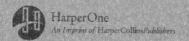

HarperOne
An Imprint of HarperCollins*Publishers*

Excerpts from *The Allegory of Love: A Study in Medieval Tradition* (Oxford: Oxford University Press, 1936) used by permission of the publisher.

Excerpts from *Christian Reflections* (Grand Rapids, MI: Wm. B. Eerdmans, 1967) and *God in the Dock*, edited by Walter Hooper (Grand Rapids, MI: William B. Eerdmans Publishing Company, 1970) used by permission of the publisher.

Excerpts from *Selected Literary Essays*, edited by Walter Hooper (Cambridge: Cambridge University Press, 1969); *Spenser's Images of Life* (Cambridge: Cambridge University Press, reissued 2013); *Studies in Medieval and Renaissance Literature* (Cambridge: Cambridge University Press, 1966, 1998, 2013); and *Studies in Words*, 2nd edition (Cambridge: Cambridge University Press, 1960, 1967, 2013) used by permission of the publisher.

Excerpts from works published by HarperOne used by permission of the publisher.

HarperCollins books may be purchased for educational, business, or sales promotional use. For information, please email the Special Markets Department at SPsales@harpercollins.com.

FIRST EDITION

Designed by Kyle O'Brien

Library of Congress Cataloging-in-Publication Data has been applied for.

ISBN 978-0-06-327644-4

22 23 24 25 26   LSC   10 9 8 7 6 5 4 3 2 1

CONTENTS

PREFACE

C. S. LEWIS PUBLISHED NEARLY FORTY BOOKS IN HIS lifetime, most of which are still in print. Apart from his Narnia Chronicles, which have sold over one hundred million copies, Lewis distinguished himself in many genres—science fiction, literary criticism, theology, memoir, and poetry. So when Lewis took time to comment on the art of writing, his observations are well worth considering.

As he became increasingly renowned in his later years, Lewis was inundated with letters on just about every topic imaginable—from spiritual direction to Spinoza to spelling. He did his best to answer as many letters as he could, though this became an onerous task. Lewis explained to one correspondent that he had answered thirty-five letters that day; on a different occasion, he noted that he had spent fourteen hours that day catching up on his correspondence (*CL* 2, 509; 3, 1153).

Lewis was a diligent reader of writing samples submitted to him, both from close friends and from complete strangers. He offered not only general evaluative remarks, but also comments on specific lines and particular word choices. Sometimes he replied by offering a quick primer on the art of writing. To a little girl from Florida he wrote, "Don't use adjectives which merely tell us how you want us to *feel* about the thing you are describing." Here, Lewis goes on to say that the writing should *delight* readers, not just label an event "delightful"; or it should make them feel *terror*, not just tell them that an event was "terrifying." He says that emotional labeling is really just a way of asking readers, "Please will you do my job for me?" (*CL* 3, 766).

Lewis recommended these same principles to many other correspondents, as well as in his published books. He frequently emphasized that one's writing should be simple, clear, concrete, and jargon-free. He also reiterated that one should *show*, not *tell*, that writers should capture sensory impressions and evoke emotions instead of simply offering an emotional label for what the reader is supposed to feel.

Lewis also believed that one should always write for the ear as well as for the eye. He recommended that a piece of prose be read aloud to make sure that its sounds reinforce its sense. In discussing Greek and Latin texts, he said it wasn't enough to work out the literal meaning of the lines; the translator should also recognize the "sound and savor of the language" (*CL* 1, 422).

Most certainly, Lewis felt the same way about English prose. To his friend Arthur Greeves, for example, he defined style as "the art of expressing a given thought in the most beautiful words and rhythms of words." To illustrate, he offered first this phrase:

"When the constellations which appear at early morning joined in musical exercises and the angelic spirits loudly testified to their satisfaction." Then he gave the actual phrase as it appears in the King James Bible: "When the morning stars sang together and all the sons of God shouted for joy" (*CL* 1, 333).

Lewis's advice on writing is worth studying partly because he was so eminently successful in practicing what he preached. Lewis's reputation shows no sign of diminishing more than a half century after his death in 1963. His Narnia Chronicles continue as perennial bestsellers, and they have been hailed in *The Oxford Companion to Children's Literature* as "the most sustained achievement in fantasy for children by a 20th-century author." Lewis's books of popular theology continue to enjoy widespread influence and appeal. And, to many readers, turning to most contemporary critics after reading Lewis's scholarly work is like (in his own phrase) "the difference between diamonds and tinsel" (*CL* 1, 247).

Lewis was arguably one of the most lucid and readable prose stylists of the modern era. Since he would, in Chaucer's phrase, "gladly teach" the art of writing, it is a wise reader who would "gladly learn."

In referencing letters written by Lewis, I draw from the three volumes of *The Collected Letters of C. S. Lewis*, which I abbreviate as such: *CL* 1, *CL* 2, and *CL* 3.

DAVID C. DOWNING
Codirector of the Marion E. Wade Center
at Wheaton College in Illinois

ON GOOD WRITING

ADVICE TO A YOUNG WRITER

You describe your Wonderful Night very well. That is, you describe the place and the people and the night and the feeling of it all, very well—but not the *thing* itself—the setting but not the jewel. And no wonder! Wordsworth often does just the same. His *Prelude* (you're bound to read it about ten years' hence. Don't try it now, or you'll only spoil it for later reading) is full of moments in which everything except the *thing* itself is described. If you become a writer you'll be trying to describe the *thing* all your life: and lucky if, out of dozens of books, one or two sentences, just for a moment, come near to getting it across. . . .

1. Always try to use the language so as to make quite clear what you mean and make sure your sentence couldn't mean anything else.

2. Always prefer the plain direct word to the long, vague one. Don't *implement* promises, but *keep* them.

3. Never use abstract nouns when concrete ones will do. If you mean "more people died," don't say "mortality rose."

4. In writing, don't use adjectives which merely tell us how you want us to *feel* about the thing you are describing. I mean, instead of telling us a thing was "terrible," describe it so that we'll be terrified. Don't say it was "delightful": make *us* say "delightful" when we've read the description. You see, all those words, (*horrifying, wonderful, hideous, exquisite*) are only like saying to your readers, "Please will you do my job for me."

5. Don't use words too big for the subject. Don't say "infinitely" when you mean "very": otherwise

you'll have no word left when you want to talk about something *really* infinite.

Letter to Joan Lancaster, June 26, 1956 (*CL* 3)

TO ANOTHER YOUNG WRITER

It is very hard to give any general advice about writing. Here's my attempt.

1. Turn off the radio.
2. Read all the good books you can, and avoid nearly all magazines.
3. Always write (and read) with the ear, not the eye. You should hear every sentence you write as if it was being read aloud or spoken. If it does not sound nice, try again.
4. Write about what really interests you, whether it is

real things or imaginary things, and nothing else. (Notice this means that if you are interested *only* in writing you will never be a writer, because you will have nothing to write about.)

5. Take great pains to be *clear*. Remember that though you start by knowing what you mean, the reader doesn't, and a single ill-chosen word may lead him to a total misunderstanding. In a story it is terribly easy just to forget that you have not told the reader something that he needs to know—the whole picture is so clear in your own mind that you forget that it isn't the same in his.

6. When you give up a bit of work, don't (unless it is hopelessly bad) throw it away. Put it in a drawer. It may come in useful later. Much of my best work, or what I think my best, is the rewriting of things begun and abandoned years earlier.

7. Don't use a typewriter. The noise will destroy your sense of rhythm, which still needs years of training.

8. Be sure you know the meaning (or meanings) of every word you use.

Letter to Thomasine, December 14, 1959 (*CL* 3)

A GOOD STORY DOESN'T NEED A "POINT"

I'm not quite sure what you meant about "silly adventure stories without any point." If they *are* silly, then having a point won't save them. But if they are good in themselves, and if by a "point" you mean some truth about the real world which one can take *out* of the story, I'm not sure that I agree. At least, I think that *looking for* a "point" in that sense may prevent one from getting the real effect of the story in itself—like listening too hard for the words in singing which isn't meant to be listened to that way (like an anthem in a chorus). I'm not at all sure about all this, mind you: only thinking as I go along.

Letter to Phyllida, December 18, 1953 (*CL* 3)

GOOD WRITING DOES NOT NECESSARILY COME FROM A GOOD HEART

"The shocking truth is that, while insincerity may be fatal to good writing, sincerity, of itself, never taught anyone to write well."

The other thing we must not say is that Bunyan wrote well because he was a sincere, forthright man who had no literary affectations and simply said what he meant. I do not doubt that is the account of the matter that Bunyan would have given himself. But it will not do. If it were the real explanation, then every sincere, forthright, unaffected man could write as well. But most people of my age learned from censoring the letters of the troops, when we were subalterns in the First War, that unliterary people, however sincere and forthright in their talk, no sooner take a pen in hand than cliché and platitude flow from it. The shocking truth is that, while insincerity may be fatal to good writing, sincerity, of itself, never taught anyone to write well. It is a moral virtue, not a literary talent. We may hope it is rewarded in a better world: it is not rewarded on Parnassus.[1]

"The Vision of John Bunyan," *Selected Literary Essays*

WAYS TO MURDER WORDS

"The greatest cause of verbicide is the fact that most people are obviously far more anxious to express their approval and disapproval of things than to describe them."

Verbicide, the murder of a word, happens in many ways. Inflation is one of the commonest; those who taught us to say *awfully* for "very," *tremendous* for "great," *sadism* for "cruelty," and *unthinkable* for "undesirable" were verbicides. Another way is verbiage, by which I here mean the use of a word as a promise to pay

---

1 Parnassus: mountain in Greece, mythical home of the Muses

which is never going to be kept. The use of *significant*
as if it were an absolute, and with no intention of ever
telling us what the thing is significant of, is an example.
So is *diametrically* when it is used merely to put *opposite*
into the superlative. Men often commit verbicide because
they want to snatch a word as a party banner, to appropriate its "selling quality." Verbicide was committed when
we exchanged *Whig* and *Tory* for *Liberal* and *Conservative*.
But the greatest cause of verbicide is the fact that most
people are obviously far more anxious to express their approval and disapproval of things than to describe them.
Hence the tendency of words to become less descriptive
and more evaluative; then to become evaluative, while
still retaining some hint of the sort of goodness or bad-
ness implied; and to end up by being purely evaluative—
useless synonyms for *good* or for *bad*. . . .

I am not suggesting that we can by an archaizing
purism repair any of the losses that have already occurred. It may not, however, be entirely useless to re-
solve that we ourselves will never commit verbicide. If

modern critical usage seems to be initiating a process which might finally make *adolescent* and *contemporary* mere synonyms for *bad* and *good*—and stranger things have happened—we should banish them from our vocabulary. I am tempted to adapt the couplet we see in some parks:

Let no one say, and say it to your shame,
That there was meaning here before you came.

Introduction, *Studies in Words*

THE POWER OF STYLE

You have started the question of prose style in your letter and ask whether it is anything more than the "literal meaning of the words." On the contrary, it means less—it means the words themselves. For every thought can be expressed in a number of different ways: and style is the art of expressing a given thought in the most beautiful words and rhythms of words. For instance, a man might say, "When the constellations which appear at early morning joined in musical exercises and the angelic spirits loudly testified to their satisfaction." Expressing exactly the same thought, the Authorized [King James] Version says, "When the morning stars sang together and all the sons of God shouted for joy." Thus by the power of style, what was nonsense becomes ineffably beautiful.

Letter to Arthur Greeves, August 4, 1917 (*CL* 1)

IMITATION AND ORIGINALITY

This is one of the privileges of art, that all things are in common: imitation, if it is forgotten, matters not, and, if it lives, is justified and does not diminish the originality of the borrower. The notion of literary property was brought by philistines[2] from the valley

---

2 philistines: those with no interest in art or culture

of the gorribeen-men[3] into Helicon[4] where it has no weight nor meaning. All poetry is one, and I love to see the great notes repeated. Homer and Virgil wrote lines not for their own works alone but for the use of all their followers. A plague on these moderns scrambling for what they call originality—like men trying to lift themselves off the earth by pulling at their own braces [suspenders]: as if by shutting their eyes to the work of the masters they were likely to create new things themselves.

Letter to Arthur Greeves, August 7, 1920 (*CL* 1)

THE PARADOX OF ORIGINALITY

No man who values originality will ever be original. But try to tell the truth as you see it, try to do any bit

---

3 gorribeen-men: moneylenders
4 Helicon: home of the Muses

of work as well as it can be done for the work's sake, and what men call originality will come unsought.

"Membership," *The Weight of Glory*

HOW TO DEVELOP A STYLE

The way for a person to develop a style is (a) to know exactly what he wants to say, and (b) to be sure he is saying exactly that. The reader, we must remember, does not start by knowing what we mean. If our words are ambiguous, our meaning will escape him. I sometimes think that writing is like driving sheep down a road. If there is any gate open to the left or the right, the readers will most certainly go into it.

"Cross-Examination," *God in the Dock*

SUITING THE STYLE TO YOUR READERS

About precocity, this isn't a change in my style. I have always had two ways of writing, one for the people (to be used in works of popularized theology) and one that never aimed at simplicity (in scholarly or imaginative works). I don't think I could, or ought, to write romances and fantasies in the style of my broadcast talks. And I'm impenitent about *dindle*. You saw at once what it meant and so I've added a lovely word to your vocabulary. Why do you object?

Letter to Mrs. E. L. Baxter, August 19, 1947 (*CL* 2)

PRACTICE, PRACTICE, PRACTICE

What you want is practice, practice, practice. It doesn't matter what we write (at least this is my view) at our age, so long as we write continually as well as we can.

I feel that every time I write a page either of prose or of verse, with real effort, even if it's thrown into the fire the next minute, I am so much further on.

Letter to Arthur Greeves, June 14, 1916 (*CL* 1)

It is impossible to write one's best if nobody else ever has a look at the result.

Letter to Arthur Greeves, June 20, 1916 (*CL* 1)

LET READERS TASTE FOR THEMSELVES

Poetry most often communicates emotions, not directly, but by creating imaginatively the grounds for those emotions. It therefore communicates something more than emotion; only by means of that something more does it communicate the emotion at all. . . .

This, which is eminently true of poetry, is true

14

of all imaginative writing. One of the first things we have to say to a beginner who has brought us his manuscript is, "Avoid all epithets which are merely emotional. It is no use *telling* us that something was 'mysterious' or 'loathsome' or 'awe-inspiring' or 'voluptuous.' Do you think your readers will believe you just because you say so? You must go quite a different way to work. By direct description, by metaphor and simile, by secretly evoking powerful associations, by offering the right stimuli to our nerves (in the right degree and the right order), and by the very beat and vowel-melody and length and brevity of your sentences, you must bring it about that we, we readers, not you, exclaim 'how mysterious!' or 'loathsome' or whatever it is. Let me taste for myself, and you'll have no need to *tell* me how I should react to the flavor."

"At the Fringe of Language," *Studies in Words*

THE MORE ABSTRACT THE TOPIC, THE LESS ABSTRACT THE PROSE

I hope this doesn't all sound too pedantic. But the matter is important. So many people, when they begin "research," lose all desire, and presently all power, of writing clear, sharp, and unambiguous English. Hold on to your finite transitive verb, your concrete nouns, and the *muscles* of language (*but, though, for, because* etc.). The more abstract the subject, the more our language should avoid all unnecessary abstraction. Write mysteriously and elusively about a drawing room if you please: but write about mysteries as like Cobbett (or Hume) as you can!

Letter to Francis Warner, July 15, 1959 (*CL* 3)

FAULTS IN UNDERGRADUATE LITERARY ESSAYS

The faults I find in contemporary undergraduate criticism are these: (1) In adverse criticism their tone is that of personal resentment. They are more anxious to wound the author than to inform the reader. Adverse criticism should diagnose and exhibit faults, not abuse them. (2) They are far too ready to advance or accept radical reinterpretations of works which have already been before the world for several generations. The *prima facie* improbability that those have never till now been understood is ignored. (3) Most European literature was composed for adult readers who knew the Bible and the classics. It is not the modern student's fault that he lacks this background; but he is insufficiently aware of his lack and of the necessity for extreme caution which it imposes on him. He should think twice before discovering "irony" in passages which everyone has hitherto taken "straight." (4) He approaches literature with the wrong kind of seriousness. He uses as a substitute for religion or philosophy or psychotherapy works which were intended as *divertissements*. The nature of the comic is a subject for serious consideration; but one needs to have seen the joke and taken it as a joke first. Of course none of these critical vices are peculiar to undergraduates. They imitate that which, in their elders, has far less excuse.

Letter to the *Cambridge Broadsheet*, March 9, 1960 (*CL* 3)

ON PLAGIARISM

I only once detected a pupil offering me someone else as his own work. I told him I was not a detective nor even a schoolmaster, nor a nurse, and that I absolutely refused to take any precaution against this puerile trick: that I'd as soon think it my business to see that he washed behind his ears or wiped his bottom. He went down of his own accord the next week and I never saw him again. I think you ought to make a general announcement of that sort. . . .

What staggers me is how any man can prefer the galley-slave labor of transcription to the freeman's work of attempting an essay on his own.

Letter to Alastair Fowler, December 10, 1959 (*CL* 3)

ON THE WRITING PROCESS

INK IS THE GREAT CURE

Whenever you are fed up with life, start writing: ink is the great cure for all human ills, as I have found out long ago.

Letter to Arthur Greeves, May 30, 1916 (*CL* 1)

INK IS A DEADLY DRUG

Ink is a deadly drug. One wants to write. I cannot shake off the addiction.

Letter to Martyn Skinner, October 11, 1950 (*CL* 3)

THE FREEDOM TO WRITE WHATEVER ONE WANTS

There is one comfort which must inevitably be wanting anywhere except at home—namely, the ability to write whenever one wishes. For, though of course there is no formal obstacle, you will readily see that it is impossible to take out one's manuscript and start to work in another's house. And, when ideas come flowing upon me, so great is the desire of framing them into words, words into sentences, and sentences into meter, that the inability to do so is no light affliction.

Letter to Arthur Greeves, November 4, 1914 (*CL* 1)

SOME ARE BORN TO WRITE

I am sure that some are born to write as trees are born to bear leaves: for these, writing is a necessary mode of their own development. If the impulse to write survives the hope of success, then one is among these. If not, then the impulse was at best only pardonable vanity, and it will certainly disappear when the hope is withdrawn.

Letter to Arthur Greeves, August 28, 1930 (*CL* 1)

WRITING IS LIKE SCRATCHING AN ITCH

As to the reward for printed work (apart from money), one's first good reviews *are* very sweet—perhaps dangerously so—and fame has *one* really solid good about it in so far as it makes some strangers approach you with a friendliness they would not have felt otherwise. It may even win you their prayers (as I hope I have yours: you certainly have mine). The rest is all in the order of those things which it is painful to miss but not really very nice to get. (It is painful not to be able to scratch a place in the middle of one's back, yet scratching doesn't rank very high among our pleasures).

Letter to Vera Gebbert, July 16, 1953 (*CL* 3)

ACADEMIC WRITING VS. IMAGINATIVE WRITING

Academic work and imaginative writing are incompatible only in the same sense as playing the piano and taking hot baths: i.e. they can't be done at the same time.

Letter to Alastair Fowler, May 19, 1955 (*CL* 3)

THE AUTHOR WITHIN VS. THE WHOLE PERSON

"There are usually two reasons for writing an imaginative work, which may be called author's reason and the man's. If only one of these is present, then, so far as I am concerned, the book will not be written. If the first is lacking, it can't; if the second is lacking, it shouldn't."

In the sixteenth century when everyone was saying that poets (by which they meant all imaginative writers) ought "to please and instruct," Tasso made a valuable distinction. He said that the poet, as poet, was concerned solely with pleasing. But then every poet was also a man and a citizen; in that capacity he ought to, and would wish to, make his work edifying as well as pleasing.

Now I do not want to stick very close to the renaissance ideas of "pleasing" and "instructing." Before I could accept either term it might need so much redefining that what was left of it at the end would not be worth retaining. All I want to use is the distinction between the author as author and the author as man, citizen, or Christian. What this comes to for me is that there are usually two reasons for writing an imaginative work, which may be called author's reason and the man's. If only one of these is present, then, so far as I am concerned, the book will not be written. If the first is lacking, it can't; if the second is lacking, it shouldn't.

In the author's mind there bubbles up every now and then the material for a story. For me it invariably begins with mental pictures. This ferment leads to nothing unless it is accompanied with the longing for a form: verse or prose, short story, novel, play, or whatnot. When these two things click you have the author's impulse complete. It is now a thing inside him pawing to get out. He longs to see that bubbling stuff pouring into that form as the cook longs to see the new jam pouring into the clean jam jar. This nags him all day long and gets in the way of his work and his sleep and his meals. It's like being in love.

While the author is in this state, the man will of course have to criticize the proposed book from quite a different point of view. He will ask how the gratification of this impulse will fit in with all the other things he wants, and ought to do or be. Perhaps the whole thing is too frivolous and trivial (from the man's point of view, not the author's) to justify the time and pains it would involve. Perhaps it would be unedifying when it was done. Or else perhaps (at this point the author cheers up) it looks like being "good," not in a merely literary sense, but "good" all around.

This may sound rather complicated but it is really very like what happens about other things. You are attracted by a girl; but is she the sort of girl you'd be wise, or right, to marry? You would like to have lobster for lunch; but does it agree with you and is it wicked to spend that amount of money on a meal? The author's impulse is a desire (it is very like an itch), and of course, like every other desire, needs to be criticized by the whole man.

Let me now apply this to my own fairy tales. Some people seem to think that I began by asking myself how I could say something about Christianity to children; then fixed on the fairy tale as an instrument; then collected information about child psychology and decided what age group I'd write for; then drew up a list of basic Christian truths and hammered out "allegories" to embody them. This is all pure moonshine. I couldn't write in that way at all. Everything began with images: a faun carrying an umbrella, a queen on a sledge, a magnificent lion. At first there wasn't even anything Christian about them; that element pushed itself in of its own accord. It was part of the bubbling.

Then came the form. As these images sorted themselves into events (i.e., became a story) they seemed to demand no love interest and no close psychology. But the form which excludes these things is the fairy tale. And the moment I thought of that I fell in love with the form itself: its brevity, its severe restraints on description, its flexible traditionalism, its inflexible hostility to all analysis, digression, reflections, and "gas." I was now enamored of it. Its very limitations of vocabulary became an attraction, as the hardness of the stone pleases the sculptor or the difficulty of the sonnet delights the sonneteer.

On that side (as author) I wrote fairy tales because the fairy tale seemed the ideal form for the stuff I had to say.

Then of course the man in me began to have his turn. I thought I saw how stories of this kind could steal past a certain inhibition which had paralyzed much of my own religion in childhood. Why did one find it so hard to feel as one was told one ought to feel about God or about the sufferings of Christ? I thought the chief reason was that one was told one ought to. An obligation to feel can freeze feelings. And reverence itself did harm. The whole subject was associated with lowered voices, almost as if it were something medical. But supposing that by casting all these things into an imaginary world, stripping them of their stained-glass and Sunday school associations, one could make them for the first time appear in their real potency? Could one not thus steal past those watchful dragons? I thought one could.

That was the man's motive. But of course he could have done nothing if the author had not been on the boil first.

You will notice that I have throughout spoken of fairy tales, not "children's stories." Professor J. R. R. Tolkien in *The Lord of the Rings* has shown that the connection between fairy tales and children is not nearly so close as publishers and educationalists think. Many children don't like them and many adults do.

The truth is, as he says, that they are now associated with children because they are out of fashion with adults; have in fact retired to the nursery as old furniture used to retire there, not because the children had begun to like it but because their elders had ceased to like it.

I was therefore writing "for children" only in the sense that I excluded what I thought they would not like or understand; not in the sense of writing what I intended to be below adult attention. I may of course have been deceived, but the principle at least saves one from being patronizing. I never wrote down to anyone; and whether the opinion condemns or acquits my own work, it certainly is my opinion that a book worth reading only in childhood is not worth reading even then. The inhibitions which I hoped my stories would overcome in a child's mind may exist in a grown-up's mind too, and may perhaps be overcome by the same means.

The fantastic or mythical is a mode available at all ages for some readers; for others, at none. At all ages, if it is well used by the author and meets the right reader, it has the same power: to generalize while remaining concrete, to present in palpable form not concepts or even experiences but whole classes of experience, and to throw off irrelevancies. But at its best it can do more; it can give us experiences we have never had and thus instead of "commenting on life," can add to it. I am speaking, of course, about the thing itself, not my own attempts at it.

"Juveniles," indeed! Am I to patronize sleep because children sleep sound? Or honey because children like it?

"Sometimes Fairy Stories May Say Best What's to Be Said," *Of Other Worlds*

WRITING IS LIKE A LUST

But to speak of the craft itself, I would not know how to advise a man how to write. It is a matter of talent and interest. I believe he must be strongly moved if he is to become a writer. Writing is like a "lust," or like "scratching when you itch." Writing comes as a result of a very strong impulse, and when it does come, I for one must get it out.

"Heaven, Earth, and Outer Space," *Decision* II, 1963

WRITING IS LIKE BUILDING A NEST

The bee builds its cell and the bird its nest, probably with no knowledge of what purpose they will serve: another sees to that. Nobody knows what the result of your writing, or mine . . . will be. But I think we may depend upon it that endless and devoted work on an object to which a man feels seriously impelled will *tell* somewhere or other: himself or others, in this world or others, will reap a harvest proportional to the output.

Letter to Arthur Greeves, August 28, 1930 (*CL* 1)

MOTIVES FOR WRITING

As for the real motives for writing after one has "got over" the desire for acknowledgment: in the first place, I found and find, that precisely at the moment when you have really put all that out of your mind and decided not to write again—or if you do, to do it with the clear consciousness that you are only playing yourself—precisely then the ideas—which came so rarely in the days when you regarded yourself officially as an author—begin to bubble and simmer, and sooner or later you will *have* to write: and the question *why* won't really enter your mind.

Letter to Arthur Greeves, August 28, 1930 (*CL* 1)

WRITING AS VICARIOUS EXPERIENCE

You ask me whether I have ever been in love: fool as I am, I am not quite such a fool as all that. But if one is only to talk from firsthand experience on any subject, conversation would be a very poor business. But though I have no personal experience of the thing they call love, I have what is better—the experience of Sappho, of Euripides, of Catullus, of Shakespeare, of Spenser, of Austen, of Brontë, of, of—anyone else I have read. We see through their eyes. And as the greater includes the less, the passion of a great mind includes all the qualities of the passion of a small one. Accordingly, we have every right to talk about it.

Letter to Arthur Greeves, October 12, 1915 (*CL* 1)

HUMAN AUTHORS ARE NOT TRULY "CREATIVE"

"Creation" as applied to human authorship . . . seems
to me an entirely misleading term. We make ἐξ
ὑποκειμένων [with regard to what lies at hand], i.e.
we rearrange elements He has provided. There is not
a *vestige* of real creativity de novo [entirely new] in
us. Try to imagine a new primary color, a third sex,
a fourth dimension, or even a monster which does
not consist of bits of existing animals stuck together!
Nothing happens. And that surely is why our works
(as you said) never mean to others quite what we intended: because we are recombining elements made
by Him and already containing *His* meanings. Because of those divine meanings in our materials it is
impossible we should ever know the whole meaning
of our own works, and the meaning we never intended
may be the best and truest one.

Writing a book is much less like creation than it is
like planting a garden or begetting a child: in all three

cases we are only entering as *one* cause into a causal stream which works, so to speak, in its own way. I would not wish it to be otherwise. If one could *really* create in the strict sense, would one not find one had created a sort of Hell?

Letter to Sister Penelope, February 20, 1943 (*CL* 2)

ON HIS OWN STRUGGLES WITH REDUNDANCY

Why can I never say anything *once*? ("Two and two make four. These pairs, in union, generate quaternity, and the duplication of duplicates leaves us one short of five.") Well, all's one. Plague of these pickled herrings!

Letter to Owen Barfield, May 17, 1943 (*CL* 2)

WRITING AND THINKING AS A SINGLE PROCESS

"I once asked [Lewis] how he managed to write with such ease, and I think his answer tells us more about his writing than anything else he said. He told me that the thing he most loved about writing was that it did two things at once. This he illustrated by saying: 'I don't know what I *mean* till I see what I've *said*.' In other words writing and thinking were a single process."

Walter Hooper, Preface to *CL* 3

RETURNING TO A WRITING TASK

Returning to work on an interrupted story is not like returning to work on a scholarly article. Facts, however long the scholar has left them untouched in his notebook, will still prove the same conclusions; he has only to start the engine running again. But the story is an organism: it goes on surreptitiously growing or decaying while your back is turned. If it decays, the resumption of work is like trying to coax back to life an almost extinguished fire, or to recapture the confidence of a shy animal which you had only partially tamed at your last visit.

English Literature in the Sixteenth Century (Excluding Drama)

DEFINING TERMS

Unless we are writing a dictionary, or a textbook of some technical subject, we define our words only because we are in some measure departing from their real current sense.

Introduction, *Studies in Words*

THE LIMITS OF LANGUAGE

Language exists to communicate whatever it can communicate. Some things it communicates so badly that we never attempt to communicate them by words if any other medium is available.

"At the Fringe of Language," *Studies in Words*

ON WRITING TO FRIENDS

After all, what is the object of writing to friends except that of talking oneself into a state of self-importance and the belief that one's own perversities are a matter of universal sympathy.

Letter to Leo Baker, September 25, 1920 (*CL* 1)

ON WRITING FICTION

CHARACTERIZATION IN ROMANCE STORIES

Just as a lobster wears its skeleton outside, so the
characters in romance wear their character outside.
For it is their story that is their character.

"The Misery of Florimel," *Spenser's Images of Life*

STORIES WITH PLOT AND STORIES WITH "ATMOSPHERE"

"In life and art both, as it seems to me, we are always
trying to catch in our net of successive moments something that is not successive."

It is astonishing how little attention critics have paid to story considered in itself. Granted the story, the style in which it should be told, the order in which it should be disposed, and (above all) the delineation of the characters, have been abundantly discussed. But the story itself, the series of imagined events, is nearly always passed over in silence, or else treated exclusively as affording opportunities for the delineation of character. . . .

It seems to me that in talking of books which are "mere stories"—books, that is, which concern themselves principally with the imagined event and not with character or society—nearly everyone makes the assumption that "excitement" is the only pleasure they ever give or are intended to give. *Excitement*, in this sense, may be defined as the alternate tension and appeasement of imagined anxiety. This is what I think untrue. In some such books, and for some readers, another factor comes in. . . .

If to love story is to love excitement, then I ought

to be the greatest lover of excitement alive. But the fact is that what is said to be the most "exciting" novel in the world, *The Three Musketeers*, makes no appeal to me at all. The total lack of atmosphere repels me. There is no country in the book—save as a storehouse of inns and ambushes. There is no weather. When they cross to London there is no feeling that London differs from Paris. There is not a moment's rest from the "adventures": one's nose is kept ruthlessly to the grindstone. It all means nothing to me. . . .

Shall I be thought whimsical if, in conclusion, I suggest that this internal tension in the heart of every story between the theme and the plot constitutes, after all, its chief resemblance to life? If story fails in that way, does not life commit the same blunder? In real life, as in a story, something must happen. That is just the trouble. We grasp at a state and find only a succession of events in which the state is never quite embodied. The grand idea of finding Atlantis which stirs us in the first chapter of the adventure story is apt to be frittered away in mere excitement when the journey has once been begun. But so, in real life, the idea of adventure fades when the day-to-day details begin to happen. Nor is this merely because actual hardship and danger shoulder it aside. Other grand ideas—homecoming, reunion with a beloved—similarly elude our grasp. Suppose there is no disappointment; even so—well, you are here. But now, something must happen, and after that something else. All that happens may be delightful: but can any such series quite embody the sheer state of being which was what we wanted? If the author's plot is only a net, and usually an imperfect one, a net of time and event for catching what is not really a process at all, is life much more? I am not sure, on second thoughts, that the slow fading of the magic in *The Well at the World's End* is, after all, a blemish. It is an image of the truth. Art, indeed, may be expected to do what life cannot do: but so it has done. The bird has escaped us. But it was at least entangled in the net for several chapters. We saw it close and enjoyed the plumage. How many "real lives" have nets that can do as much?

In life and art both, as it seems to me, we are always trying to catch in our net of successive moments something that is not successive. Whether in real life there is any doctor who can teach us how to do it, so that at last either the meshes will become fine enough to hold the bird, or we be so changed that we can throw our nets away and follow the bird to its own country, is not a question for this essay. But I think it is sometimes done—or very, very nearly done—in stories. I believe the effort to be well worth making.

"On Stories," *Of Other Worlds*

REALISTIC DRIVEL IN MODERN FICTION

It is a strange comment on our age that such a book lies hid in a hideous paper-backed edition, wholly unnoticed by the cognoscenti, while any "realistic" drivel about some neurotic in a London flat—something that needs no real invention at all, something that any educated man could write if he chose—may get seriously reviewed and mentioned in serious books, as if it really mattered. I wonder how long this tyranny will last? Twenty years ago I felt no doubt that I should live to see it all break up and great literature return: but here I am, losing teeth and hair, and still no break in the clouds.

Letter to Joy Gresham, December 22, 1953 (*CL* 3)

SURPRISES MAY FADE, BUT "SURPRISINGNESS" LASTS

"We do not enjoy a story fully at the first reading. Not till the curiosity, the sheer narrative lust, has been given its sop and laid asleep, are we at leisure to savor the real beauties."

An unliterary man may be defined as one who reads books once only. There is hope for a man who has never read Malory or Boswell or *Tristram Shandy* or Shakespeare's *Sonnets*: but what can you do with a man who says he 'has read' them, meaning he has read them once, and thinks that this settles the matter? . . . For excitement . . . is just what must disappear from a second reading. You cannot, except at the first reading, be really curious about what happened. If you find that the reader of popular romance—however uneducated a reader, however bad the romances—goes back to his old favorites again and again, then you have pretty good evidence that they are to him a sort of poetry.

The re-reader is looking not for actual surprises (which can come only once) but for a certain surprisingness. The point has often been misunderstood. . . . We do not enjoy a story fully at the first reading. Not till the curiosity, the sheer narrative lust, has been given its sop and laid asleep, are we at leisure to savor the real beauties. Till then, it is like wasting great wine on a ravenous natural thirst which merely wants cold wetness. The children understand this well when they ask for the same story over and over again, and in the same words. They want to have again the 'surprise' of discovering that what seemed Little-Red-Riding-Hood's grandmother is really the wolf. It is better when you know it is coming: free from the shock of actual surprise you can attend better to the intrinsic surprisingness of the *peripeteia*.

Note: *Peripeteia*: plot structure

"On Stories," *Of Other Worlds*

ON WRITING POETRY

Great subjects do not make great poems;
usually, indeed, the reverse.

—English Literature in the Sixteenth Century
(Excluding Drama)

A THRILL LIKE MUSIC

Isn't it funny the way some combinations of words can
give you—almost apart from their meaning—a thrill
like music?

Letter to Arthur Greeves, March 21, 1916 (*CL* 1)

THE METER AND THE MAGIC OF POETIC LANGUAGE

You are quite right when you talk about thinking more of the matter than of the form. All I meant when I talked about the importance of form was to carry a little further what you already feel in prose—that is how some phrases such as "the wall of the world," or "at the back of the north wind" affect you, partly by sound, partly by association, more than the same meaning would if otherwise expressed. The only difference is that poetry makes use of that sort of feeling much more than prose and produces those effects by meter as well as by phrase. In fact, the meter and the magic of the words should be like the orchestration of a Wagnerian opera—should sort of fill the matter by expressing things that can't be directly told—that is, it expresses feeling while the matter expresses thought.

Letter to Arthur Greeves, July 11, 1916 (*CL* 1)

POETRY FOR THE LIPS AS WELL AS THE EYES

By the way, I most fully agree with you about "the lips being invited to share the banquet" in poetry, and always "mouth" it while I read, though not in a way that would be audible to other people in the room. (Hence the excellent habit which I once formed, but have since lost, of not smoking while reading a poem.) I look upon this "mouthing" as an infallible mark of those who really like poetry. Depend upon it, the man who reads verses in any other way, is after "noble thoughts" or "philosophy" (in the revolting sense given to that word by Browning societies and Aunt Lily) or social history, or something of the kind, not poetry.

Letter to his brother, Warren Lewis, April 8, 1932 (*CL* 2)

JOHN SKELTON'S PERFECTION IN LIGHT POETRY

[Skelton's] "Philip Sparrow" is our first great poem of childhood. . . . It is indeed the lightest—the most like a bubble—of all the poems I know. It would break at a touch: but hold your breath, watch it, and it is almost perfect. The Skeltonics are essential to its perfection. Their prattling and hopping and their inconsequence, so birdlike and so childlike, are the best possible embodiment of the theme. We should not, I think, refuse to call this poem great; perfection in light poetry, perfect smallness, is among the rarest of literary achievements.

English Literature in the Sixteenth Century (Excluding Drama)

POETRY AS AN INCARNATION OF THOUGHT

It seems to me appropriate, almost inevitable, that when that great Imagination which in the beginning, for Its own delight and for the delight of men and angels and (in their proper mode) of beasts, had invented and formed the whole world of Nature, submitted to express Itself in human speech, that speech should sometimes be poetry. For poetry too is a little incarnation, giving body to what had been before invisible and inaudible.

Reflections on the Psalms

POETRY AS A MODE OF WRITING

When what the poet is saying is religious, poetry is simply a part of religion. When what he says is simply entertaining, poetry is a form of entertainment. When what he says is wicked, poetry is simply a form of sin. Whenever one is talking, if one begins to utilize rhythm, metaphor, association, etc., one is beginning to use "poetry": but the whole place of that poetry in the scheme of things depends on what you are talking about. In fact, in a sense there is no such thing as poetry. It is not an element but a *mode*.

Letter to Dom Bede Griffiths, July 28, 1936 (*CL* 2)

ON POLITICAL POETRY

The real parallel to much modern political poetry is not religious poetry concerned with God or the Passion or Heaven but merely pious poetry concerned with (ugh!) "religion." The religion of politics is a religion without sacraments: for the human sacrifices which it practices are mere murder, not even ritual murder. Wordsworth compensated for the (poetically) ghost-like nature of politics by using a strict form, the sonnet. But that *matter*, with vers libre [free verse] as the form, is to me quite unpardonable: a noisy vacuity.

Letter to Chad Walsh, October 20, 1950 (*CL* 3)

ON WRITING FOR CHILDREN

"I am almost inclined to set it up as a canon that a children's story which is enjoyed only by children is a bad children's story. The good ones last. A waltz which you can like only when you are waltzing is a bad waltz."

I think there are three ways in which those who write for children may approach their work: two good ways and one that is generally a bad way.

I came to know of the bad way quite recently and from two unconscious witnesses. One was a lady who sent me the manuscript of a story she had written in which a fairy placed at a child's disposal a wonderful gadget. I say "gadget" because it was not a magic ring or hat or cloak or any such traditional matter. It was a machine, a thing of taps and handles and buttons you could press. You could press one and get an ice cream, another and get a live puppy, and so forth. I had to tell the author honestly that I didn't much care for that sort of thing. She replied, "No more do I, it bores me to distraction. But it is what the modern child wants." My other bit of evidence was this. In my own first story I had described at length what I thought a rather fine high tea given by a hospitable faun to the little girl who was my heroine. A man, who has children of his own, said, "Ah, I see how you got to that. If you want to please grown-up readers you give them sex, so you thought to yourself, 'That won't do for children, what shall I give them instead? I know! The little blighters like plenty of good eating.'" In reality, however, I myself like eating and drinking. I put in what I would have liked to read when I was a child and what I still like reading now that I am in my fifties.

The lady in my first example, and the married man in my second, both conceived writing for children as a special department of "giving the public what it wants." Children are, of course, a special public and you find out what they want and give them that, however little you like it yourself.

The next way may seem at first to be very much the same, but I think the resemblance is superficial. This is the way of Lewis Carroll, Kenneth Grahame, and Tolkien. The printed story grows out of a story told to a particular child with the living voice and perhaps extempore. It resembles the first way because you are certainly trying to give that child what it wants. But then you are dealing with a concrete person; this child who, of course, differs from all other children. There is no question of "children" conceived as a strange species whose habits you have "made up" like an anthropologist or a commercial traveler. Nor, I suspect, would it be possible, thus face to face, to regale the child with things calculated to please it but regarded by yourself with indifference or contempt. The child, I am certain, would see through that. In any personal relation, the two participants modify each other. You would become slightly different because you were talking to a child and the child would become slightly different because it was being talked to by an adult. A community, a composite personality, is created and of that the story grows.

The third way, which is the only one I could ever use myself, consists in writing a children's story because a children's story is the best art form for something you have to say: just as a composer might write a dead march not because there was a public funeral in view but because certain musical ideas that had occurred to him went best into that form. This method could apply to other kinds of children's literature besides stories. I have been told that Arthur Mee never met a child and never wished to: it was, from his point of view, a bit of luck that boys liked reading what he liked writing. This anecdote may be untrue in fact but it illustrates my meaning.

Within the species "children's story" the subspecies which happened to suit me is the fantasy or (in a loose sense of that word) the fairy tale. There are, of course, other subspecies. E. Nesbit's trilogy about the Bastable family is a very good specimen of another kind. It is a "children's story" in the sense that children can and do read it: but it is also the only form in which E. Nesbit could have given us so much of the humors of childhood. It is true that the Bastable children appear, successfully treated from the adult point of view, in one of her grown-up novels, but they appear only for a moment. I do not think she would have kept it up. Sentimentality is so apt to creep in if we write at length about children as seen by their elders. And the reality of childhood, as we all experienced it, creeps out. For we all remember that our childhood, as lived, was immeasurably different from what our elders saw. Hence Sir Michael Sadler, when I asked his opinion about a certain new experimental school, replied, "I never give an opinion on any of those experiments till the children have grown up and can tell us *what really happened*." Thus the Bastable trilogy, however improbable many of its episodes may be, provides even adults, in one sense, with more realistic reading about children than they could find in most books addressed to adults. But also, conversely, it enables the children who read it to do something much more mature than they realize. For the whole book is a character study of Oswald, an unconsciously satiric self-portrait, which every intelligent child can fully appreciate: but no child would sit down to read a character study in any other form. There is another way in which children's stories mediate this psychological interest, but I will reserve that for later treatment.

In this short glance at the Bastable trilogy I think we have stumbled on a principle. Where the children's story is simply the right form for what the author has to say, then of course readers who want to hear that, will read the story or reread it, at any age. I never met *The Wind in the Willows* or the Bastable books till

I was in my late twenties, and I do not think I have enjoyed them any the less on that account. I am almost inclined to set it up as a canon that a children's story which is enjoyed only by children is a bad children's story. The good ones last. A waltz which you can like only when you are waltzing is a bad waltz.

This canon seems to me most obviously true of that particular type of children's story which is dearest to my own taste, the fantasy or fairy tale. Now the modern critical world uses *adult* as a term of approval. It is hostile to what it calls *nostalgia* and contemptuous of what it calls *Peter Pantheism*. Hence a man who admits that dwarfs and giants and talking beasts and witches are still dear to him in his fifty-third year is now less likely to be praised for his perennial youth than scorned and pitied for arrested development. If I spend some little time defending myself against these charges, this is not so much because it matters greatly whether I am scorned and pitied as because the defense is germane to my whole view of the fairy tale and even of literature in general. My defense consists of three propositions.

1. I reply with a tu quoque ["you also," i.e. you have the same problem]. Critics who treat *adult* as a term of approval, instead of as a merely descriptive term, cannot be adult themselves. To be concerned about being grown up, to admire the grown-up because it is grown up, to blush at the suspicion of being childish: these things are the marks of childhood and adolescence. And in childhood and adolescence they are, in moderation, healthy symptoms. Young things ought to want to grow. But to carry on into middle life or even into early manhood this concern about being adult is a mark of really arrested development. When I was ten, I read fairy tales in secret and would have been ashamed if I had been found doing so. Now that I am fifty I read them openly. When I became a man I put away childish things, including the fear of childishness and the desire to be very grown up.

2. The modern view seems to me to involve a false

conception of growth. They accuse us of arrested development because we have not lost a taste we had in childhood. But surely arrested development consists not in refusing to lose old things but in failing to add new things? I now like hock [white wine], which I am sure I should not have liked as a child. But I still like lemon squash. I call this growth or development because I have been enriched: where I formerly had only one pleasure, I now have two. But if I had to lose the taste for lemon squash before I acquired the taste for hock, that would not be growth but simple change. I now enjoy Tolstoy and Jane Austen and Trollope as well as fairy tales and I call that growth: if I had had to lose the fairy tales in order to acquire the novelists, I would not say that I had grown but only that I had changed. A tree grows because it adds rings: a train doesn't grow by leaving one station behind and puffing on to the next. In reality, the case is stronger and more complicated than this. I think my growth is just as apparent when I now read the fairy tales as when I read the novelists, for I now enjoy the fairy tales better than I did in childhood: being now able to put more in, of course I get more out. But I do not here stress that point. Even if it were merely a taste for grown-up literature added to an unchanged taste for children's literature, addition would still be entitled to the name "growth," and the process of merely dropping one parcel when you pick up another would not. It is, of course, true that the process of growing does, incidentally and unfortunately, involve some more losses. But that is not the essence of growth, certainly not what makes growth admirable or desirable. If it were, if to drop parcels and to leave stations behind were the essence and virtue of growth, why should we stop at the adult? Why should not *senile* be equally a term of approval? Why are we not to be congratulated on losing our teeth and hair? Some critics seem to confuse growth with the cost of growth and also to wish to make that cost far higher than, in nature, it need be.

3. The whole association of fairy tale and fantasy with childhood is local and accidental. I hope everyone has read Tolkien's essay on fairy tales, which is perhaps the most important contribution to the subject that anyone has yet made. If so, you will know already that, in most places and times, the fairy tale has not been specially made for, nor exclusively enjoyed by, children. It has gravitated to the nursery when it became unfashionable in literary circles, just as unfashionable furniture gravitated to the nursery in Victorian houses. In fact, many children do not like this kind of book, just as many children do not like horsehair sofas: and many adults do like it, just as many adults like rocking chairs. And those who do like it, whether young or old, probably like it for the same reason. And none of us can say with any certainty what that reason is. The two theories which are most often in my mind are those of Tolkien and of Jung.

According to Tolkien the appeal of the fairy story lies in the fact that man there most fully exercises his function as a "subcreator"; not, as they love to say now, making a "comment upon life" but making, so far as possible, a subordinate world of his own. Since, in Tolkien's view, this is one of man's proper functions, delight naturally arises whenever it is successfully performed. For Jung, fairy tale liberates archetypes which dwell in the collective unconscious, and when we read a good fairy tale we are obeying the old precept "Know thyself." I would venture to add to this my own theory, not indeed of the kind as a whole, but of one feature in it: I mean, the presence of beings other than human which yet behave, in varying degrees, humanly: the giants and dwarfs and talking beasts. I believe these to be at least (for they may have many other sources of power and beauty) an admirable hieroglyphic which conveys psychology, types of character, more briefly than novelistic presentation and to readers whom novelistic presentation could not yet reach. Consider Mr. Badger in *The Wind in the Willows*—that extraordinary amalgam of high rank, coarse manners, gruffness, shyness, and good-ness. The child who has once met Mr. Badger has ever afterward, in its bones, a knowledge of humanity and of English social history which it could not get in any other way.

Of course as all children's literature is not fantastic, so all fantastic books need not be children's books. It is still possible, even in an age so ferociously anti-romantic as our own, to write fantastic stories for adults: though you will usually need to have made a name in some more fashionable kind of literature before anyone will publish them. But there may be an author who at a particular moment finds not only fan-tasy but fantasy-for-children the exactly right form for what he wants to say. The distinction is a fine one. His fantasies for children and his fantasies for adults will have very much more in common with one another than either has with the ordinary novel or with what is sometimes called "the novel of child life." Indeed the same readers will probably read both his fantastic "juveniles" and his fantastic stories for adults. For I need not remind such an audience as this that the neat sorting out of books into age groups, so dear to publishers, has only a very sketchy relation with the habits of any real readers. Those of us who are blamed when old for reading childish books were blamed when children for reading books too old for us. No reader worth his salt trots along in obedience to a timetable. The distinction, then, is a fine one: and I am not quite sure what made me, in a particular year of my life, feel that not only a fairy tale, but a fairy tale addressed to children, was exactly what I must write——or burst. Partly, I think, that this form permits, or compels, you to leave out things I wanted to leave out. It compels you to throw all the force of the book into what was done and said. It checks what a kind but discerning critic called "the expository demon" in me. It also imposes certain very fruitful necessities about length.

If I have allowed the fantastic type of children's story to run away with this discussion, that is because it is the kind I know and love best, not because I wish to condemn any other. But the patrons of the other kinds very frequently want to condemn it. About once every hundred years some wiseacre gets up and tries to banish the fairy tale. Perhaps I had better say a few words in its defense, as reading for children.

It is accused of giving children a false impression of the world they live in. But I think no literature that children could read gives them less of a false impression. I think what profess to be realistic stories for children are far more likely to deceive them. I never expected the real world to be like the fairy tales. I think that I did expect school to be like the school stories. The fantasies did not deceive me: the school stories did. All stories in which children have adventures and successes which are possible, in the sense that they do not break the laws of nature, but almost infinitely improbable, are in more danger than the fairy tales of raising false expectations.

Almost the same answer serves for the popular

charge of escapism, though here the question is not so simple. Do fairy tales teach children to retreat into a world of wish fulfillment—"fantasy" in the technical psychological sense of the word—instead of facing the problems of the real world? Now it is here that the problem becomes subtle. Let us again lay the fairy tale side by side with the school story or any other story which is labeled a "boy's book" or a "girl's book," as distinct from a "children's book." There is no doubt that both arouse, and imaginatively satisfy, wishes. We long to go through the looking glass, to reach fairy land. We also long to be the immensely popular and successful schoolboy or schoolgirl, or the lucky boy or girl who discovers the spy's plot or rides the horse that none of the cowboys can manage. But the two longings are very different. The second, especially when directed on something so close as school life, is ravenous and deadly serious. Its fulfillment on the level of imagination is in very truth compensatory: we run to it from the disappointments and humiliations of the real world; it sends us back to the real world un-divinely discontented. For it is all flattery to the ego. The pleasure consists in picturing oneself the object of admiration. The other longing, that for fairy land, is very different. In a sense a child does not long for fairy land as a boy longs to be the hero of the first eleven [varsity soccer players]. Does anyone suppose that he really and prosaically longs for all the dangers and discomforts of a fairy tale?—really wants drag-ons in contemporary England? It is not so. It would be much truer to say that fairy land arouses a longing for he knows not what. It stirs and troubles him (to his lifelong enrichment) with the dim sense of something beyond his reach and, far from dulling or emptying the actual world, gives it a new dimension of depth. He does not despise real woods because he has read of enchanted woods: the reading makes all real woods a little enchanted. This is a special kind of longing. The boy reading the school story of the type I have in mind desires success and is unhappy (once the book is over) because he can't get it: the boy reading the fairy tale desires and is happy in the very fact of desiring. For his mind has not been concentrated on himself, as it often is in the more realistic story.

I do not mean that school stories for boys and girls ought not to be written. I am only saying that they are far more liable to become "fantasies" in the clinical sense than fantastic stories are. And this distinction holds for adult reading too. The dangerous fantasy is always superficially realistic. The real victim of wishful reverie does not batten on the *Odyssey*, *The Tempest*, or *The Worm Ouroboros*: he (or she) prefers stories about millionaires, irresistible beauties, posh hotels, palm beaches, and bedroom scenes—things that really might happen, that ought to happen, that would have happened if the reader had had a fair chance. For, as I say, there are two kinds of longing. The one is an *ascesis*, a spiritual exercise, and the other is a disease.

A far more serious attack on the fairy tale as children's literature comes from those who do not wish children to be frightened. I suffered too much from night fears myself in childhood to undervalue this objection. I would not wish to heat the fires of that private hell for any child. On the other hand, none of my fears came from fairy tales. Giant insects were my specialty, with ghosts a bad second. I suppose the ghosts came directly or indirectly from stories, though certainly not from fairy stories, but I don't think the insects did. I don't know anything my parents could have done or left undone which would have saved me from the pincers, mandibles, and eyes of those many-legged abominations. And that, as so many people have pointed out, is the difficulty. We do not know what will or will not frighten a child in this particular way. I say "in this particular way" for we must here make a distinction. Those who say that children must not be frightened may mean two things. They may mean (1) that we must not do anything likely to give the child those haunting, disabling, pathological fears against which ordinary courage is helpless: in fact, *phobias*. His mind must, if possible, be kept clear of things he can't bear to think of. Or they may mean (2) that we must try to keep out of his mind the knowledge that he is born into a world of death, violence, wounds, adventure, heroism and cowardice, good and evil. If they mean the first, I agree with them: but not if they mean the second. The second would indeed be to give children a false impression and feed them on escapism in the bad sense. There is something ludicrous in the idea of so educating a generation which is born to the OGPU [Soviet secret police] and the atomic bomb. Since it is so likely that they will meet cruel enemies, let them at least have heard of brave knights and heroic courage. Otherwise you are making their destiny not brighter but darker. Nor do most of us find that violence and bloodshed, in a story, produce any haunting dread in the minds of children. As far as that goes, I side impenitently with the human race against the modern reformer. Let there be wicked kings and beheadings, battles and dungeons, giants and dragons, and let villains be soundly killed at the end of the book. Nothing will persuade me that this causes an ordinary child any kind or degree of fear beyond what it wants, and needs, to feel. For, of course, it wants to be a little frightened.

The other fears—the phobias—are a different matter. I do not believe one can control them by literary means. We seem to bring them into the world with us ready-made. No doubt the particular image on which the child's terror is fixed can sometimes be traced to a book. But is that the source, or only the occasion, of the fear? If he had been spared that image, would not some other, quite unpredictable by you, have had the same effect? Chesterton has told us of a boy who was more afraid of the Albert Memorial than anything else in the world. I know a man whose great childhood terror was the India paper edition of the *Encyclopedia Britannica*—for a reason I defy you to guess. And I think it possible that by confining your child to blameless stories of child life in which nothing at all alarming ever happens, you would fail to banish the terrors, and would succeed in banishing all that can ennoble them or make them endurable. For in the fairy tales, side by side with the terrible figures, we find the immemorial comforters and protectors, the radiant ones; and the terrible figures are not merely terrible, but sublime. It would be nice if no little boy in bed, hearing, or thinking he hears, a sound, were ever at all frightened. But if he is going to be frightened, I think it better that he should think of giants and dragons than merely of burglars. And I think Saint George, or any bright champion in armor, is a better comfort than the idea of the police.

I will even go further. If I could have escaped all my own night fears at the price of never having known "faeries," would I now be the gainer by that bargain? I am not speaking carelessly. The fears were very bad. But I think the price would have been too high.

But I have strayed far from my theme. This has

been inevitable for, of the three methods, I know by experience only the third. I hope my title did not lead anyone to think that I was conceited enough to give you advice on how to write a story for children. There were two very good reasons for not doing that. One is that many people have written very much better stories than I, and I would rather learn about the art than set up to teach it. The other is that, in a certain sense, I have never exactly "made" a story. With me the process is much more like bird-watching than like either talking or building. I see pictures. Some of these pictures have a common flavor, almost a common smell, which groups them together. Keep quiet and watch and they will begin joining themselves up. If you were very lucky (I have never been as lucky as all that) a whole set might join themselves so consistently that there you had a complete story: without doing anything yourself. But more often (in my experience always) there are gaps. Then at last you have to do some deliberate inventing, have to contrive reasons why these characters should be in these various places doing these various things. I have no idea whether this is the usual way of writing stories, still less whether it is the best. It is the only one I know: images always come first.

Before closing, I would like to return to what I said at the beginning. I rejected any approach which begins with the question "What do modern children like?" I might be asked, "Do you equally reject the approach which begins with the question 'What do modern children need?'—in other words, with the moral or didactic approach?" I think the answer is yes. Not because I don't like stories to have a moral: certainly not because I think children dislike a moral. Rather because I feel sure that the question "What do modern children need?" will not lead you to a good moral. If we ask that question we are assuming too superior an attitude. It would be better to ask "What moral do I need?" for I think we can be sure that what does not concern us deeply will not deeply interest our readers, whatever their age. But it is better not to ask the question at all. Let the pictures tell you their own moral. For the moral inherent in them will rise from whatever spiritual roots you have succeeded in striking during the whole course of your life. But if they don't show you any moral, don't put one in. For the moral you put in is likely to be a platitude, or even a falsehood, skimmed from the surface of your consciousness. It is impertinent to offer the children that. For we have been told on high authority that in the moral sphere they are probably at least as wise as we. Anyone who *can* write a children's story without a moral, had better do so: that is, if he is going to write children's stories at all. The only moral that is of any value is that which arises inevitably from the whole cast of the author's mind.

Indeed everything in the story should arise from the whole cast of the author's mind. We must write for children out of those elements in our own imagination which we share with children: differing from our child readers not by any less, or less serious, interest in the things we handle, but by the fact that we have other interests which children would not share with us. The matter of our story should be a part of the habitual furniture of our minds. This, I fancy, has been so with all great writers for children, but it is not generally understood. A critic not long ago said in praise of a very serious fairy tale that the author's tongue "never once got into his cheek." But why on earth should it?—unless he had been eating a seedcake. Nothing seems to me more fatal, for this art, than an idea that whatever we share with children is, in the privative sense, "childish" and that whatever is childish is somehow comic. We must meet children as equals in that area of our nature where we are their equals. Our superiority consists partly in commanding other areas, and partly (which is more relevant) in the fact that we are better at telling stories than they are. The child as reader is neither to be patronized nor idolized: we talk to him as man to man. But the worst attitude of all would be the professional attitude which regards children in the lump as a sort of raw material which we have to handle. We must of course try to do them no harm: we may, under the Omnipotence, sometimes dare to hope that we may do them good. But only such good as involves treating them with respect. We must not imagine that we are Providence or Destiny. I will not say that a good story for children could never be written by someone in the Ministry of Education, for all things are possible. But I should lay very long odds against it.

Once in a hotel dining room I said, rather too loudly, "I loathe prunes." "So do I," came an unexpected six-year-old voice from another table. Sympathy was instantaneous. Neither of us thought it funny. We both knew that prunes are far too nasty to be funny. That is the proper meeting between man and child as independent personalities. Of the far higher and more difficult relations between child and parent or child and teacher, I say nothing. An author, as a mere author, is outside all that. He is not even an uncle. He is a freeman and an equal, like the postman, the butcher, and the dog next door.

"On Three Ways of Writing for Children," *Of Other Worlds*

RIGHT AND WRONG WAYS OF WRITING FOR CHILDREN

"It follows that there are now two very different sorts of 'writers for children.' The wrong sort believe that children are 'a distinct race.' . . . The right sort work from the common, universally human, ground they share with the children, and indeed with countless adults."

Not long ago I saw in some periodical the statement that "Children are a distinct race." Something like this seems to be assumed today by many who write, and still more who criticize, what are called children's books or "juveniles." Children are regarded as being at any rate a distinct *literary* species, and the production of books that cater for their supposedly odd and alien taste has become an industry, almost a heavy one.

This theory does not seem to me to be borne out by the facts. For one thing, there is no literary taste common to all children. We find among them all the same types as among ourselves. Many of them, like many of us, never read when they can find any other entertainment. Some of them choose quiet, realistic, "slice-of-life" books (say, *The Daisy Chain*) as some of us choose Trollope.

Some like fantasies and marvels, as some of us like the *Odyssey*, Boiardo, Ariosto, Spenser, or Mr. Mervyn Peake. Some care for little but books of information, and so do some adults. Some of them, like some of us, are omnivorous. Silly children prefer success stories about school life as silly adults like success stories about grown-up life.

We can approach the matter in a different way by drawing up a list of books which, I am told, have been generally liked by the young. I suppose Aesop, *The Arabian Nights*, *Gulliver's Travels*, *Robinson Crusoe*, *Treasure Island*, *Peter Rabbit*, and *The Wind in the Willows* would be reasonable choices. Only the last three were written for children, and those three are read with pleasure by many adults. I, who disliked *The Arabian Nights* as a child, dislike it still.

It may be argued against this that the enjoyment by children of some books intended for their elders does not in the least refute the doctrine that there is a specifically childish taste. They select (you may say) that minority of ordinary books which happens to suit them, as a foreigner in England may select those English dishes which come nearest to suiting his alien palate. And the specifically childish taste has been generally held to be that for the adventurous and the marvelous.

Now this, you may notice, implies that we are regarding as specifically childish a taste which in many, perhaps in most, times and places has been that of the whole human race. Those stories from Greek or Norse mythology, from Homer, from Spenser, or from folklore which children (but by no means all children) read with delight were once the delight of everyone.

Even the fairy tale *proprement dit* [properly speaking] was not originally intended for children; it was told and enjoyed in (of all places) the court of Louis XIV. As Professor Tolkien has pointed out, it gravitated to the nursery when it went out of fashion among the grown-ups, just as old-fashioned furniture gravitated to the nursery. Even if all children and no adults now liked the marvelous—and neither is the case—we ought not to say that the peculiarity of children lies in their liking it. The peculiarity is that they *still* like it, even in the twentieth century.

It does not seem to me useful to say, "What delighted the infancy of the species naturally still delights the infancy of the individual." This involves a parallel between individual and species which we are in no position to draw. What age is man? Is the race now in its childhood, its maturity, or its dotage? As we don't know at all exactly when it began, and have no notion when it will end, this seems a nonsense question. And who knows if it will ever be mature? Man may be killed in infancy.

Surely it would be less arrogant, and truer to the evidence, to say that the peculiarity of child readers is that they are not peculiar. It is we who are peculiar. Fashions in literary taste come and go among the adults, and every period has its own shibboleths. These, when good, do not improve the taste of children, and, when bad, do not corrupt it; for children read only to enjoy. Of course their limited vocabulary and general ignorance make some books unintelligible to them. But apart from that, juvenile taste is simply human taste, going on from age to age, silly with a universal silliness or wise with a universal wisdom, regardless of modes, movements, and literary revolutions.

This has one curious result. When the literary establishment—the approved canon of taste—is so extremely jejune and narrow as it is today, much has to be addressed in the first instance to children if it is to get printed at all. Those who have a story to tell must appeal to the audience that still cares for storytelling.

The literary world of today is little interested in the narrative art as such; it is preoccupied with technical novelties and with "ideas," by which it means not literary, but social or psychological, ideas. The ideas (in the literary sense) on which Miss Norton's *The Borrowers* or Mr. White's *Mistress Masham's Repose* are built would not need to be embodied in "juveniles" at most periods.

It follows that there are now two very different sorts of "writers for children." The wrong sort believe that children are "a distinct race." They carefully "make up" the tastes of these odd creatures—like an anthropologist observing the habits of a savage tribe—or even the tastes of a clearly defined age group within a particular social class within the "distinct race." They dish up not what they like themselves but what that race is supposed to like. Educational and moral, as well as commercial, motives may come in.

The right sort work from the common, universally human, ground they share with the children, and indeed with countless adults. They label their books "for children" because children are the only market now recognized for the books they, anyway, want to write.

"On Juvenile Tastes," *Of Other Worlds*

"MAKING UP IS A VERY MYSTERIOUS THING."

"All my seven Narnian books, and my three science-fiction books, began with seeing pictures in my head. At first they were not a story, just pictures."

The editor has asked me to tell you how I came to write *The Lion, the Witch, and the Wardrobe*. I will try, but you must not believe all that authors tell you about how they wrote their books. This is not because they mean to tell lies. It is because a man writing a story is too excited about the story itself to sit back and notice how he is doing it. In fact, that might stop the works; just as, if you start thinking about how you tie your tie, the next thing is that you find you can't tie it. And afterward, when the story is finished, he has forgotten a good deal of what writing it was like.

One thing I am sure of. All my seven Narnian books, and my three science-fiction books, began with seeing pictures in my head. At first they were not a story, just pictures. *The Lion* all began with a picture of a faun carrying an umbrella and parcels in a snowy wood. This picture had been in my mind since I was about sixteen. Then one day, when I was about forty, I said to myself: "Let's try to make a story about it."

At first I had very little idea how the story would

go. But then suddenly Aslan came bounding into it. I think I had been having a good many dreams of lions about that time. Apart from that, I don't know where the Lion came from or why He came. But once He was there He pulled the whole story together, and soon He pulled the six other Narnian stories in after Him.

So you see that, in a sense, I know very little about how this story was born. That is, I don't know where the pictures came from. And I don't believe anyone knows exactly how he "makes things up." Making up is a very mysterious thing. When you "have an idea," could you tell anyone exactly *how* you thought of it?

"It All Began with a Picture . . . ," *Of Other Worlds*

ON WRITING
SCIENCE FICTION

ON SCIENCE FICTION / FANTASY AS ESCAPIST

About "escapism," never let that flea stick in your ear. I was liberated from it once and for all when a friend said, "These critics are very sensitive to the least hint of escape. Now what class of men would one expect to be thus worked up about escape?—*jailers*." Turnkey critics: people who want to keep the world in some ideological prison because a glimpse at any remote prospect would make their stuff seem less exclusively important.

Fantasy and science fiction is by miles the best.

Some of the most serious satire of our age appears in it. What is called "serious" literature now—Dylan Thomas and Pound and all that—is really the most frivolous.

Letter to Arthur C. Clarke, January 26, 1954 (*CL* 3)

DON'T WASTE THE EXOTIC LOCATION IN A SCIENCE-FICTION NOVEL

With K. Neville's *She Knew He Was Coming* we touch rock bottom. The old theme of the sentimentalized brothel and the whore with a heart of gold is mawkish anyway, but tolerable; but what, in heaven's name, is the point of locating it on Mars? Surely in a work of art all the material should be *used*. If a theme is introduced into a symphony, something must be made of that theme. If a poem is written in a certain meter, the particular qualities of that meter must be exploited. If you write a historical novel, the *period* must be essential to the effect. For whatever in art is not doing good is doing harm: no room for passengers. (In a good black-and-white drawing the areas of white paper are essential to the whole design, just as much as the lines. It is only in a child's drawing that they're *merely* blank paper.) What's the excuse for locating one's story on Mars unless "Martianity" is through and through *used*?[1]

Letter to Arthur C. Clarke, January 20, 1954 (*CL* 3)

ADVICE TO A BUDDING SCIENCE-FICTION NOVELIST

I hope you will not think it impertinent if I mention (this is only one man's opinion, of course) some mistakes you can avoid in future.

1 Emotionally and atmospherically *as well as* logically [Lewis's note]

1. In all stories which take one to another world, the difficulty (as you and I know) is to make something happen when we've got there. In fact, one needs "filling." Yours is quite sufficient in *quantity* (almost too much) but not quite, I think, of the right sort. Aren't all these economic problems and religious differences too like the politics of our own world? Why go to faeries for what we already have? Surely the wars of faeries should be high, reckless, heroical, romantic wars—concerned with the possession of a beautiful queen or an enchanted treasure? Surely the diplomatic phase of them should be represented not by conferences (which, on your own showing, are as dull as ours) but by ringing words of gay taunt, stern defiance, or quixotic generosity, interchanged by great warriors with sword in hand before the battle joins?

2. This is closely connected with the preceding. In a fantasy every precaution must be taken never to break the spell, to do nothing which will wake

the reader and bring him back with a bump to the common earth. But this is what you sometimes do. The moving bar on which they travel is a dull invention at best, because we can't help conceiving it as mechanical. But when you add upholstered seats, lavatories, and restaurants, I can't go on believing in faeries for a moment. It has all turned into commonplace technological luxury! Similarly even a half-fairy ought not climb a fairy hill carrying a suitcase full of new nighties. All magic dies at this touch of the commonplace. (Notice, too, the disenchanting implication that the fairies can't make for themselves lingerie as good as they can get—not even in Paris, which would be bad enough, but, of all places—in London.)

3. Never use adjectives or adverbs which are mere appeals to the reader to feel as you want him to feel. He won't do it just because you ask him: you've got to *make* him. No good *telling* us a battle was "exciting." If *you* succeeded in exciting us, the ad-

jective will be unnecessary: if you don't, it will be useless. Don't tell us the jewels had an "emotional" glitter; make us feel the emotion. I can hardly tell you how important this is.

4. You are too fond of long adverbs like "dignifiedly," which are not nice to pronounce. I hope, by the way, you always write by ear not by eye. Every sentence should be tested on the tongue, to make sure that the sound of it has the hardness or softness, the swiftness or languor, which the meaning of it calls for.

5. Far less about clothes, please! I mean, ordinary clothes. If you had given your fairies strange and beautiful clothes and described *them*, there might be something in it. But your heroine's tangerine skirt! For whom do you write? No *man* wants to hear how she was dressed, and the sort of woman who does seldom reads fantasy: if she reads anything it is more likely to be the women's magazines.

By the way, these are a baneful influence on your mind and imagination. Beware! They may kill your talent. If you *can't* keep off them, at least, after each debauch, give your imagination a good mouthwash by reading (or would it be rereading) the *Odyssey*, Tolkien's *Lord of the Rings*, E. R. Eddison's *The Worm Ouroboros*, the romances of James Stephens, and all the early mythical plays of W. B. Yeats. Perhaps a touch of Lord Dunsany too.

6. Names not too good. They ought to be beautiful and suggestive as well as strange: not merely odd like *Enaj* (which sounds as if it came out of Butler's *Erewhon*).

7. I hope all this does not enrage you. You'll get so much bad advice that I felt I must give you some of what I think good.

Letter to Jane Gaskell, September 2, 1957 (*CL* 3)

GOOD AND BAD TYPES OF SCIENCE-FICTION STORIES

"I am, then, condemning not all books which suppose a future widely different from the present, but those which do so without a good reason, which leap a thousand years to find plots and passions which they could have found at home."

Sometimes a village or small town which we have known all our lives becomes the scene of a murder, a novel, or a centenary, and then for a few months everyone knows its name and crowds go to visit it. A like thing happens to one's private recreations. I had been walking, and reading Trollope, for years when I found myself suddenly overtaken, as if by a wave from behind, by a boom in Trollope and a short-lived craze for what was called hiking. And lately I have had the same sort of experience again. I had read fantastic fiction of all sorts ever since I could read, including, of course, the particular kind which Wells practiced in his *Time Machine*, *First Men in the Moon*, and others. Then, some fifteen or twenty years ago, I became aware of a bulge in the production of such stories. In America whole magazines began to be exclusively devoted to them. The execution was usually detestable; the conceptions, sometimes worthy of better treatment. About this time the name *scientifiction*, soon altered to *science fiction*, began to be common. Then, perhaps five or six years ago, the bulge still continuing and even increasing, there was an improvement: not that very bad stories ceased to be the majority, but that the good ones became better and more numerous. It was after this that the *genre* began to attract the attention (always, I think, contemptuous) of the literary weeklies. There seems, in fact, to be a double paradox in its history: it began to be popular when it least deserved popularity, and to excite critical contempt as soon as it ceased to be wholly contemptible.

Of the articles I have read on the subject (and I

expect I have missed many) I do not find that I can make any use. For one thing, most were not very well informed. For another, many were by people who clearly hated the kind they wrote about. It is very dangerous to write about a kind you hate. Hatred obscures all distinctions. I don't like detective stories and therefore all detective stories look much alike to me: if I wrote about them, I should therefore infallibly write drivel. Criticism of kinds, as distinct from criticism of works, cannot of course be avoided: I shall be driven to criticize one subspecies of science fiction myself. But it is, I think, the most subjective and least reliable type of criticism. Above all, it should not masquerade as criticism of individual works. Many reviews are useless because, while purporting to condemn the book, they only reveal the reviewer's dislike of the kind to which it belongs. Let bad tragedies be censured by those who love tragedy, and bad detective stories by those who love the detective story. Then we shall learn their real faults. Otherwise we shall find epics blamed for not being novels, farces for not being high comedies, novels by James for lacking the swift action of Smollett. Who wants to hear a particular claret abused by a fanatical teetotaler, or a particular woman by a confirmed misogynist? . . .

I will now try to divide this species of narrative [science fiction] into its subspecies. I shall begin with that subspecies which I think radically bad, in order to get it out of our way.

In this subspecies the author leaps forward into an imagined future when planetary, sidereal, or even galactic travel has become common. Against this huge backcloth he then proceeds to develop an ordinary love story, spy story, wreck story, or crime story. This seems to me tasteless. Whatever in a work of art is not used, is doing harm. The faintly imagined, and sometimes strictly unimaginable, scene and properties only blur the real theme and distract us from any interest it might have had. I presume that the authors of such stories are, so to speak, displaced persons—

commercial authors who did not really want to write science fiction at all, but who availed themselves of its popularity by giving a veneer of science fiction to their normal kind of work. But we must distinguish. A leap into the future, a rapid assumption of all the changes which are feigned to have occurred, is a legitimate "machine" if it enables the author to develop a story of real value which could not have been told (or not so economically) in any other way. . . . *Brave New World* and *1984* leap to our minds. I can see no objection to such a "machine." Nor do I see much use in discussing, as someone did, whether books that use it can be called "novels" or not. That is merely a question of definition. You may define the novel either so as to exclude or so as to include them. The best definition is that which proves itself most convenient. And of course to devise a definition for the purpose of excluding either *The Waves* in one direction or *Brave New World* in another, and then blame them for being excluded, is foolery.

I am, then, condemning not all books which suppose a future widely different from the present, but those which do so without a good reason, which leap a thousand years to find plots and passions which they could have found at home.

Having condemned that subspecies, I am glad to turn to another which I believe to be legitimate, though I have not the slightest taste for it myself. If the former is the fiction of the displaced persons, this might be called the fiction of engineers. It is written by people who are primarily interested in space travel, or in other undiscovered techniques, as real possibilities in the actual universe. They give us in imaginative form their guesses as to how the thing might be done. Jules Verne's *Twenty Thousand Leagues Under the Sea* and Wells's *Land Ironclads* were once specimens of this kind, though the coming of the real submarine and the real tank has altered their original interest. Arthur Clarke's *Prelude to Space* is another. I am too uneducated scientifically to criticize such stories on the mechanical side; and I am so completely out of sympathy with the projects they anticipate that I am incapable of criticizing them as stories. I am as blind to their appeal as a pacifist is to *Maldon* and *Lepanto*, or an aristocratophobe (if I may coin the word) to the *Arcadia*. But heaven forbid that I should regard the limitations of my sympathy as anything save a red light which warns me not to criticize at all. For all I know, these may be very good stories in their own kind.

I think it useful to distinguish from these engineers' stories a third subspecies where the interest is, in a sense, scientific, but speculative. When we learn from the sciences the probable nature of places or conditions which no human being has experienced, there is, in normal men, an impulse to attempt to imagine them. Is any man such a dull clod that he can look at the moon through a good telescope without asking himself what it would be like to walk among those mountains under that black, crowded sky? The scientists themselves, the moment they go beyond purely mathematical statements, can hardly avoid describing the facts in terms of their probable effect on the senses of a human observer. Prolong this, and give, along with that observer's sense experience, his probable emotions and thoughts, and you at once have a rudimentary science fiction. And of course men have been doing this for centuries. What would Hades be like if you could go there alive? Homer sends Odysseus there and gives his answer. Or again, what would it be like at the antipodes? (For this was a question of the same sort so long as men believed that the torrid zone rendered them forever inaccessible.) Dante takes you there: he describes with all the gusto of the later scientifictionist how surprising it was to see the sun in such an unusual position. Better still, what would it be like if you could get to the center of the earth? Dante tells you at the end of the *Inferno* where he and Virgil, after climbing down from the shoulders to the waist of Lucifer, find that they have to climb up from his waist to his feet, because of course they have passed the center of gravitation. It is a perfect science-fiction effect. Thus again Athanasius Kircher in his *Iter Extaticum Celeste* (1656) will take you to all the planets and most of the stars, presenting as vividly as he can what you would see and feel if this were possible. He, like Dante, uses supernatural means of transport. In Wells's *First Men in the Moon* we have means which are feigned to be natural. What keeps his story within this subspecies, and distinguishes it from those of the engineers, is his choice of a quite impossible composition called cavorite. This impossibility is of course a merit, not a defect. A man of his ingenuity could easily have thought up something more plausible. But the more plausible, the worse. That would merely invite interest in actual possibilities of reaching the moon, an interest foreign to his story. Never mind how they got there; we are imagining what it would be like. The first glimpse of the unveiled airless sky, the lunar landscape, the lunar levity, the incomparable solitude, then the growing terror, finally the overwhelming approach of the lunar night—it is for these things that the story (especially in its original and shorter form) exists.

How anyone can think this form illegitimate or contemptible passes my understanding. It may very well be convenient not to call such things novels. If you prefer, call them a very special form of novels. Either way, the conclusion will be much the same: they are to be tried by their own rules. It is absurd to condemn them because they do not often display any deep or sensitive characterization. They oughtn't to. It is a fault if they do. Wells's Cavor and Bedford have rather too much than too little character. Every good writer knows that the more unusual the scenes and events of his story are, the slighter, the more ordinary, the more typical his persons should be. Hence Gulliver is a commonplace little man and Alice a commonplace little girl. If they had been more remarkable they would have wrecked their books. The ancient mariner himself is a very ordinary man. To tell how odd things struck odd people is to have an oddity too much: he who is to see strange sights must not himself be strange. He ought to be as nearly as possible as Everyman or Anyman. Of course, we must not confuse slight or typical characterization with impossible or unconvincing characterization. Falsification of character will always spoil a story. But character can apparently be reduced, simplified, to almost any extent with wholly satisfactory results. The greater ballads are an instance.

Of course, a given reader may be (some readers seem to be) interested in nothing else in the world except detailed studies of complex human personalities. If so, he has a good reason for not reading those kinds of work which neither demand nor admit it. He has no reason for condemning them, and indeed no qualification for speaking of them at all. We must not allow the novel of manners to give laws to all literature: let it rule its own domain. We must not listen to Pope's maxim about the proper study of mankind. The proper study of man is everything. The proper study of man as artist is everything which gives a foothold to the imagination and the passions. . . .

My next subspecies is what I would call the eschatological. It is about the future, but not in the same way as *Brave New World* or *The Sleeper Awakes*. They were political or social. This kind gives an imaginative vehicle to speculations about the ultimate destiny of our species. Examples are Wells's *Time Machine*, Olaf Stapledon's *Last and First Men*, or Arthur Clarke's *Childhood's End*. It is here that a definition of science fiction which separates it entirely from the novel becomes imperative. The form of *Last and First Men* is not novelistic at all. It is indeed in a new form—the pseudo history. The pace, the concern with broad, general movements, the tone, are all those of the historiographer, not the novelist. It was the right form for the theme. And since we are here diverging so widely from the novel, I myself would gladly include in this subspecies a work which is not even narrative,

Geoffrey Dennis's *The End of the World* (1930). And I would certainly include, from J. B. S. Haldane's *Possible Worlds* (1927), the brilliant, though to my mind depraved, paper called "The Last Judgment." . . .

I turn at last to that subspecies in which alone I myself am greatly interested. It is best approached by reminding ourselves of a fact which every writer on the subject whom I have read completely ignores. Far the best of the American magazines bears the significant title *Fantasy and Science Fiction*. In it (as also in many other publications of the same type) you will find not only stories about space travel but stories about gods, ghosts, ghouls, demons, fairies, monsters, etc. This gives us our clue. The last subspecies of science fiction represents simply an imaginative impulse as old as the human race working under the special conditions of our own time. It is not difficult to see why those who wish to visit strange regions in search of such beauty, awe, or terror as the actual world does not supply have increasingly been driven to other planets or other stars. It is the result of increasing geographical knowledge. The less known the real world is, the more plausibly your marvels can be located near at hand. As the area of knowledge spreads, you need to go further afield: like a man moving his house further and further out into the country as the new building estates catch him up. Thus in Grimm's *Märchen*, stories told by peasants in wooded country, you need only walk an hour's journey into the next forest to find a home for your witch or ogre. . . . By the eighteenth century we have to move well out into the country. Paltock and Swift take us to remote seas, Voltaire to America. Rider Haggard had to go to unexplored Africa or Tibet; Bulwer-Lytton, to the depths of the earth. It might have been predicted that stories of this kind would, sooner or later, have to leave Tellus altogether. . . .

In this kind of story the pseudoscientific apparatus is to be taken simply as a "machine" in the sense which that word bore for the neoclassical critics. The most superficial appearance of plausibility—the merest sop to our critical intellect—will do. I am inclined to think that frankly supernatural methods are best. I took a hero once to Mars in a spaceship, but when I knew better I had angels convey him to Venus. Nor need the strange worlds, when we get there, be at all strictly tied to scientific probabilities. It is their wonder, or beauty, or suggestiveness that matter. When I myself put canals on Mars I believe I already knew that better telescopes had dissipated that old optical delusion. The point was that they were part of the Martian myth as it already existed in the common mind. . . .

In all these the impossibility is, as I have said, a postulate, something to be granted before the story gets going. Within that frame we inhabit the known world and are as realistic as anyone else. But in the next type (and the last I shall deal with) the marvelous is in the grain of the whole work. We are, throughout, in another world. What makes that world valuable is not, of course, mere multiplication of the marvelous either for comic effect (as in *Baron Munchausen* and sometimes in Ariosto and Boiardo) or for mere astonishment (as, I think, in the worst of the *Arabian Nights* or in some children's stories), but for its quality, its flavor. If good novels are comments on life, good stories of this sort (which are very much rarer) are actual additions to life; they give, like certain rare dreams, sensations we never had before, and enlarge our conception of the range of possible experience. Hence the difficulty of discussing them at all with those who refuse to be taken out of what they call "real life"—which means, perhaps, the groove through some far wider area of possible experience to which our senses and our biological, social, or economic interests usually confine us—or, if taken, can see nothing outside it but aching boredom or sickening monstrosity. They shudder and ask to go home. Specimens of this kind, at its best, will never be common. I would include parts of the *Odyssey*, the *Hymn to Aphrodite*, much of the *Kalevala* and *The Faerie Queene*, some of Malory (but none of Malory's best work) and more of *Huon*, parts of Novalis's *Heinrich von Ofterdingen*, "*The Ancient Mariner*" and *Christabel*, Beckford's *Vathek*, Morris's *Jason* and the *prologue* (little else) of the *Earthly Paradise*, MacDonald's *Phantastes*, *Lilith*, and *The Golden Key*, Eddison's *Worm Ouroboros*, Tolkien's *Lord of the Rings*, and that shattering, intolerable, and irresistible work, David Lindsay's *Voyage to Arcturus*. Also Mervyn Peake's *Titus Groan*. Some of Ray Bradbury's stories perhaps make the grade. W. H. Hodgson's *The Night Land* would have made it in eminence from the unforgettable somber splendor of the images it presents, if it were not disfigured by a sentimental and irrelevant erotic interest and by a foolish and flat archaism of style. (I do not mean that all archaism is foolish, and have never seen the modern hatred of it cogently defended. If archaism succeeds in giving us the sense of having entered a remote world, it justifies itself. Whether it is correct by philological standards does not then matter a rap.)

I am not sure that anyone has satisfactorily explained the keen, lasting, and solemn pleasure which such stories can give. Jung, who went furthest, seems to me to produce as his explanation one more myth which affects us in the same way as the rest. Surely the analysis of water should not itself be wet? I shall not attempt to do what Jung failed to do. But I would like to draw attention to a neglected fact: the astonishing intensity of the dislike which some readers feel for the mythopoeic. I first found it out by accident. A lady (and, what makes the story more piquant, she herself was a Jungian psychologist by profession) had been talking about a dreariness which seemed to be creeping over her life, the drying up in her of the power to feel pleasure, the aridity of her mental landscape. Drawing a bow at a venture, I asked, "Have you any taste for fantasies and fairy tales?" I shall never forget how her muscles tightened, her hands clenched themselves, her eyes started as if with horror, and her voice changed, as she hissed out, "I *loathe* them."

Clearly we here have to do not with a critical opinion but with something like a phobia. And I have seen traces of it elsewhere, though never quite so violent. On the other side, I know from my own experience, that those who like the mythopoeic like it with almost equal intensity. The two phenomena, taken together, should at least dispose of the theory that it is something trivial. It would seem from the reactions it produces, that the mythopoeic is rather, for good or ill, a mode of imagination which does something to us at a deep level. If some seem to go to it in almost compulsive need, others seem to be in terror of what they may meet there. But that is of course only suspicion. What I feel far more sure of is the critical *caveat* which I propounded a while ago. Do not criticize what you have no taste for without great caution. And above all, do not ever criticize what you simply can't stand. I will lay all the cards on the table. I have long since discovered my own private *phobia*, the thing I can't bear in literature, the thing which makes me profoundly uncomfortable: the representation of anything like a quasi love affair between two children. It embarrasses and nauseates me. But of course I regard this not as a charter to write slashing reviews of books in which the hated theme occurs, but as a warning not to pass judgment on them at all. For my reaction is unreasonable: such child loves quite certainly occur in real life and I can give no reason why they should not be represented in art. If they touch the scar of some early *trauma* in me, that is my misfortune. And I would venture to advise all who are attempting to become critics to adopt the same principle. A violent and actually resentful reaction to all books of a certain kind, or to situations of a certain kind, is a danger signal. For I am convinced that good adverse criticism is the most difficult thing we have to do. I would advise everyone to begin it under the most favorable conditions: this is, where you thoroughly know and heartily like the thing the author is trying to do, and have enjoyed many books where it was done well. Then you will have some chance of really showing that he has failed and perhaps even of showing why. But if our real reaction to a book is "Ugh! I just can't bear this sort of thing," then I think we shall not be able to diagnose whatever real faults it has. We may labor to conceal our emotion, but we shall end in a welter of emotive, unanalyzed, vogue words—"arch," "facetious," "bogus," "adolescent," "immature," and the rest. When we really know what is wrong, we need none of these.

"On Science Fiction," *Of Other Worlds*

ON CHRISTIAN
WRITING

SOMETIMES ONE'S FAITH SHOULD BE LATENT IN THE WRITING, NOT BLATANT

I think you have a mistaken idea of a Christian writer's duty. We must use the talent we have, not the talents we haven't. We must *not* of course write anything that will flatter lust, pride, or ambition. But we needn't all write patently moral or theological work. Indeed, work whose Christianity is latent may do quite as much good and may reach some whom the more obvious religious work would scare away.

The first business of a story is to be a *good story*.

When our Lord made a wheel in the carpenter shop, depend upon it, it was first and foremost a *good wheel*. Don't try to "bring in" specifically Christian bits: if God wants you to serve Him in that way (He may not: there are different vocations), you will find it coming in of its own accord. If not, well—a good story which will give innocent pleasure is a good thing, just like cooking a good nourishing meal. (You don't put little texts in your family soup, I'll be bound.)

By the way, none of my stories *began* with a Christian message. I always start from a mental picture— the floating islands, a faun with an umbrella in a snowy wood, an "injured" human head. Of course my nonfiction works are different. But they succeed because I'm a professional teacher, and explanation happens to be one of the things I've learned to do.

But the great thing is to cultivate one's own garden, to do well the job which one's own natural capacities point out (after first doing well whatever the "duties of one's station" impose). *Any* honest workmanship (whether making stories, shoes, or rabbit hutches) can be done to the glory of God.

Letter to Cynthia Donnelly, August 14, 1954 (*CL* 3)

THE RIGHT QUESTION TO ASK

The Christian writer: . . . if his talents are such that he can produce good work by writing in an established form and dealing with experiences common to all his race, he will do so. . . . It is to him an argument not of strength but of weakness that he should respond fully to the vision only "in his own way." And always of every idea and of every method he will ask not "Is it mine?," but "Is it good?"

"Christianity and Literature," *Christian Reflections*

WRITING CLEARLY FORCES YOU TO THINK CLEARLY

You must translate every bit of your theology into the vernacular. This is very troublesome, and it means you say very little in half an hour, but it is essential. It is also of the greatest service to your own thought. I have come to the conviction that if you cannot translate your thoughts into uneducated language, then your thoughts were confused. Power to translate is the test of having really understood one's own meaning.

"Christian Apologetics," *God in the Dock*

ON WRITING
PERSUASIVELY

JOSEPH ADDISON'S METHOD FOR UNDERMINING HIS OPPONENTS

This contrast between Addison and the Tories comes out with special clarity in their treatment of enemies. For the Tories, every enemy—whether it be the Duchess of Marlborough or only a Shakespearian editor found guilty of some real English scholarship—becomes a grotesque. All who have, in whatever fashion, incurred their ill will are knaves, scarecrows, whores, bugs, toads, bedlamites, yahoos; Addison himself a smooth Mephistopheles. It is good fun, but it is certainly not good sense; we laugh, and disbelieve. Now mark Addison's procedure. . . . With the help of Steele, he invents Sir Roger de Coverley. The measure of his success is that we can now think of Sir Roger for a long time without remembering his Toryism; when we do remember it, it is only as a lovable whimsy. . . . The enemy, far from being vilified, is being turned into a dear old man. The thought that he could ever be dangerous has been erased from our minds; but so also the thought that anything he said could ever be taken seriously.

"Addison," *Selected Literary Essays*

A DISAGREEMENT SHOULD NOT BECOME A QUARREL

What shocks me is that students, academics, men of letters, should display what I had thought was an essentially uneducated inability to differentiate between a disputation and a quarrel. The real objection to this sort of thing is that it is all a distraction from the issue. You waste on calling me liar and hypocrite time you ought to have spent on refuting my position. Even if your main purpose was to gratify resentment, you have gone about it the wrong way. Any man would much rather be called names than proved wrong.

Letter to the editors of *Delta: The Cambridge Literary Magazine*, February 1961 (*CL* 3)

ON OTHER WRITERS

JOSEPH ADDISON

All we can justly say is that his essays are rather small beer; there is no iron in them as in Johnson; they do not stir the depths. . . . Addison is, above all else, comfortable. He is not on that account to be condemned. He is an admirable cure for the fidgets.

"Addison," *Selected Literary Essays*

JANE AUSTEN

Her books have only two faults and both are damnable.
They are too few and too short.

Letter to R. W. Chapman, September 6, 1949 (*CL* 2)

FRANCIS BACON

It is a shock to turn to the *Essays*. Even the completed
Essays of 1625 is a book whose reputation curiously
outweighs any real pleasure or profit that most people
have found in it, a book (as my successor admirably
says) which "everyone has read but no one is ever
found reading." The truth is, it is a book for adoles-
cents.

Epilogue, *English Literature in the Sixteenth Century (Excluding Drama)*

ON WRITING (AND WRITERS)

EMILY BRONTË'S *JANE EYRE*

This week I have reread *Jane Eyre*. It is quite prodigiously better than the other Brontë books. I know you have never gone back to it, but I think if one omits (as I did this time) the early chapters about the school days—a senseless recording of miseries which have no effect upon the main story—it is very well worth reading. Part of the interest lies in seeing in the most (apparently) preposterous male characters how quite ordinary people look through the eyes of a shy, naive, inflexibly upright, intelligent little woman of the mouse-like governessy type. . . . Particularly delicious is her idea of conjugal bliss when she says almost on the last page, "We talk, I believe, all day." Poor husband!

Letter to his brother, Warren Lewis, November 19, 1939 (*CL* 2)

129

JOHN BUNYAN'S *PILGRIM'S PROGRESS*

I am reading at present, what do you think? Our own friend *Pilgrim's Progress*. It is one of those books that are usually read too early to appreciate, and perhaps not come back to. I am very glad however to have discovered it. The allegory of course is obvious and even childish, but just as a romance it is unsurpassed, and also as a specimen of real English. Try a bit of your Ruskin or Macaulay after it, and see the difference between diamonds and tinsel.

Letter to his father, Albert Lewis, March 11, 1916 (*CL* 1)

GEOFFREY CHAUCER

Chaucer has few rivals, and no masters.

The Allegory of Love

WILLIAM COWPER

Have you ever read the letters of the poet Cowper? He had nothing—literally nothing—to tell anyone about: private life in a sleepy country town where Evangelical distrust of "the world" denied him even such miserable society as the place would have afforded. And yet one reads a whole volume of his correspondence with unfailing interest. How his tooth came loose at dinner, how he made a hutch for a tame hare, what he is doing about his cucumbers—all this he makes one follow as if the fate of empires hung on it.

Letter to his father, Albert Lewis, February 25, 1928 (*CL* 1)

THOMAS CRANMER

Cranmer writes a prose with which it is difficult to find any fault, but it gives curiously little pleasure. It never drags and never hurries; it never disappoints the ear; and (*pace* John Foxe) there is hardly a single sentence that leaves us in doubt of its meaning. . . . The explanation is that Cranmer always writes in an official capacity. Everything he says has been threshed out in committee. We never see a thought growing: his business is to express the agreed point of view. Everyone who has tried to draw up a report knows how fatal such conditions are to good writing.

English Literature in the Sixteenth Century (Excluding Drama)

SAMUEL DANIEL

His [sonnet] sequence *Delia* . . . offers no ideas, no psychology, and of course no story: it is simply a masterpiece of phrasing and melody. To anyone who complains that it is a series of commonplaces we can only reply, "Yes, but listen." . . . In him, as in Shakespeare, the most ordinary statement turns liquid and delicious. . . . The truth is that while everything Daniel says would be commonplace in a prose abstract, nothing is commonplace as it actually occurs in the poetry. In that medium all the Petrarchan gestures become compulsive invitations to enormous sorrows and delights.

English Literature in the Sixteenth Century (Excluding Drama)

DANTE (ALIGHIERI)

Dante remains a strong candidate for the supreme poetical honors of the world.

The Allegory of Love

I think Dante's poetry, on the whole, the greatest of all the poetry I have read: yet when it is at its highest pitch of excellence, I hardly feel that Dante has very much to do. . . . I draw the conclusion that the highest reach of the whole poetic art turns out to be a kind of abdication, and is attained when the whole image of the world the poet sees has entered so deeply into his mind that henceforth he has only to get himself out of the way, to let the seas roll and the mountains shake their leaves or the light shine and the spheres revolve, and all this will *be* poetry, not things you write poetry about. Dare I confess that after Dante even Shakespeare seems to me a little factitious? It almost sounds as if he were "just making it up." But one cannot feel that about Dante even when one has stopped reading him.

"Dante's Similes," *Studies in Medieval and Renaissance Literature*

WALTER DE LA MARE

De la Mare's poems I have had for a long time and I read them more often than any other book. I put him above Yeats and all the other moderns, and in spite of his fantasy find him nearer than anyone else to the essential truth of life.

Letter to Arthur Greeves, June 26, 1927 (*CL* 1)

ALL ACTION, NO ATMOSPHERE IN *THE THREE MUSKETEERS*

One never knows how good Scott is till one tries to read Dumas. Have you noticed how completely Dumas lacks any background? In Scott, behind the adventures of the hero, you have the whole society of the age, with all the interplay of town and country, Puritan and Cavalier, Saxon and Norman, or whatnot, and all the racy humor of the minor characters: and behind that again you have the eternal things—the actual countryside, the mountains, the weather, the very *feel* of traveling. In Dumas, if you try to look even an inch behind the immediate intrigue, you find just nothing at all. You are in an abstract world of gallantry and adventure which has no *roots*—no connection with human nature or mother earth. When the scene shifts from Paris to London there is no sense that you have reached a new country, no change of atmosphere. And I don't think there is a single passage to show that Dumas had ever seen a cloud, a road, or a tree. In a word, if you were asked to explain what you and I meant by "the homely" in literature, you could almost reply, "It means the opposite of *The Three Musketeers*." But perhaps I am being too hard on what after all was written only for amusement. I suppose there must be a merit in the speed and verve of the plot, even if I don't like that kind of thing.

Letter to Arthur Greeves, March 25, 1933 (*CL* 2)

T. S. ELIOT'S "THE LOVE SONG OF J. ALFRED PRUFROCK"

I don't believe one person in a million, under any emotional stress, would see evening like that.[1] And even if they did, I believe that anything but the most sparing admission of such images is a very dangerous game. To invite them, to recur willingly to them, to come to regard them as normal, surely, poisons us?

Letter to Katharine Farrer, February 9, 1954 (*CL* 3)

T. S. ELIOT'S "THE WASTE LAND"

[T. S. Eliot's] intention only God knows. I must be content to judge his work by its fruits, and I contend

---

1 The opening lines of the poem:

> Let us go then, you and I,
> When the evening is spread out against the sky
> Like a patient etherized upon a table.

that no man is fortified against chaos by reading "The Waste Land," but that most men are by it infected with chaos.

The opposite plea rests on a very elementary confusion between poetry that represents disintegration and disintegrated poetry. The *Inferno* is not infernal poetry: "The Waste Land" is.

Letter to Paul Elmer More, May 23, 1935 (*CL* 2)

T. S. ELIOT AS A CRITIC

Oh Eliot! How can a man who is neither a knave nor a fool write so like both? Well, he can't complain that I haven't done my best to put him right—I hardly ever write a book without showing him one of his errors. And still he doesn't mend. I call it ungrateful.

Letter to Dorothy Sayers, October 23, 1942 (*CL* 2)

RALPH WALDO EMERSON

You are quite right about Emerson. I often pick him up here for an odd quarter of an hour, and go away full of new ideas. Every sentence is weighty: he puts into paragraphs what others, seeking charm, expand into whole essays or chapters. At the same time his tense concentration makes him painful reading, he gives you no rest. I don't know why you object to his style—it seems to me admirable. *Quel dommage* [What a pity] that such a man should be an American.

Letter to Arthur Greeves, September 12, 1918 (*CL* 1)

ROBERT FROST

[Robert Frost] is one of the few living poets for whom I feel something like reverence.

Letter to Basil Willey, May 23, 1957 (*CL* 3)

NATHANIEL HAWTHORNE'S *THE HOUSE OF THE SEVEN GABLES*

Although by experience I am somewhat shy of recommending books to other people, I think I am quite safe in earnestly advising you to make "the Gables" your next purchase. By the way I shouldn't have said "mystery," there is really no mystery in the proper sense of the word, but a sort of feeling of fate and inevitable horror as in [Charlotte Brontë's] *Wuthering Heights*. I really think I have never enjoyed a novel more. There is one lovely scene where the villain—Judge [Pyncheon]—has suddenly died in his chair, all alone in the house, and it describes the corpse sitting there as the day wears on and the room grows darker—darker—and the ticking of his watch. But that sort of bald description is no use! I must leave you to read that wonderful chapter to yourself. . . .

I intend to read all Hawthorne after this. What a pity such a genius should be a beastly American!

Letter to his father, Albert Lewis, November 19, 1916 (*CL* 1, 258–59)

RICHARD HOOKER

Every system offers us a model of the universe; Hooker's model has unsurpassed grace and majesty. . . . Few model universes are more filled—one might say, more drenched —with Deity than his. . . . God is unspeakably transcendent; but also unspeakably immanent. . . . The style is, for its purpose, perhaps the most perfect in English.

English Literature in the Sixteenth Century (Excluding Drama)

A. E. HOUSMAN

I also glanced through A. E. Housman's *Shropshire Lad* for the hundredth time. What a terrible little book it is—perfect and deadly, the beauty of the gorgon.

Letter to Arthur Greeves, October 6, 1929 (CL 1)

HENRY JAMES

I have just finished Volume 1 of Henry James's letters. An interesting man, though a dreadful prig: but he did appreciate Stevenson. A *phantasmal* man, who had never known God, or earth, or war, never done a day's compelled work, never had to earn a living, had no home and no duties.

Letter to Roger Lancelyn Green, October 21, 1952 (*CL* 3)

SAMUEL JOHNSON

There is no subject on which more nonsense has been talked than the style of Johnson. For me his best sentences in writing have the same feeling as his best conversation—"Pop! It was so sudden." I don't know anyone who can settle a thing so well in half a dozen words.

Letter to his brother, Warren Lewis, August 2, 1928 (*CL* 1)

KING JAMES BIBLE

I am not convinced that its rhythms (they are various) are very different from those of any good prose that is written for the most part in short sentences, nor that they would strike us as noticeably fine if divorced from their matter. "After the cocktail, a soup—but the soup was not very nice—and after the soup a small, cold pie." It is not a bad sentence: but it is very different from its rhythmical equivalent "After the earthquake, a fire; but the Lord was not in the fire: and after the fire a still small voice" (1 Kings 19:12).

English Literature in the Sixteenth Century (Excluding Drama)

RUDYARD KIPLING

Kipling is intensely loved and hated. Hardly any reader likes him a little. . . . One moment I am filled with delight at the variety and solidity of his imagination; and then, at the very next moment, I am sick, sick to death, of the whole Kipling world.

"Kipling's World," *Selected Literary Essays*

D. H. LAWRENCE

Lady Chatterley has made short work of a prosecution by the Crown.[2] It still has to face more formidable judges. Nine of them, and all goddesses.[3]

"Four-Letter Words," *Selected Literary Essays*

---

2 The novel faced charges of obscenity in British courts.
3 goddesses: the Muses

The "great literary experience" of George MacDonald's *Phantastes*

I have had a great literary experience this week. I have discovered yet another author to add to our circle—our very own set. Never since I first read *The Well at the World's End* [by William Morris] have I enjoyed a book so much—and indeed I think my new "find" is quite as good as Malory or Morris himself. The book, to get to the point, is George MacDonald's "faerie romance," *Phantastes*, which I picked up by hazard in a rather tired Everyman copy—by the way, isn't it funny, they cost 1/1d. now—on our station bookstall last Saturday. . . .

Of course it is hopeless for me to try and describe it, but when you have followed the hero Anodos along that little stream to the fairy wood, have heard about the terrible ash tree and how the shadow of his gnarled, knotted hand falls upon the book the hero is reading, when you have read about the fairy palace . . . and heard the episode of Cosmo, I know that you will quite agree with me. You must not be disappointed at the first chapter which is rather conventional fairy tale style, and after it you won't be able to stop until you have finished.

Letter to Arthur Greeves, March 7, 1916 (*CL* 1)

SPIRITUAL HEALING IN GEORGE MACDONALD

I know nothing that gives me such a feeling of spiritual healing, of being washed, as to read G. MacDonald.

Letter to Arthur Greeves, August 31, 1930 (*CL* 1)

MACHIAVELLI

It would be unreasonable . . . to pass over in silence *The Prince* (1513) of Machiavelli, for there the repudiation of medieval principles goes farthest. But for that very reason Machiavelli is not very important. He went too far. Everyone answered him, everyone disagreed with him. The book's success was a success of scandal. To readers who seriously sought instruction in the art of tyranny he could, after all, reveal only the secrets which all men knew. Not to be, but to seem, virtuous—it is a formula whose utility we all discovered in the nursery.

English Literature in the Sixteenth Century (Excluding Drama)

MODERN AMERICAN POETS

I feel as you do about modern English poetry. American is better. Lee Masters, Frost, and Robinson Jeffers all really have something to *say* and some real art.

Letter to Dom Bede Griffiths, April 22, 1954 (*CL* 3)

MODERN NOVELS

I have read nothing lately, except a foolish modern novel which I read at one sitting—or rather one lying on the sofa—this afternoon in the middle of a terrible thunderstorm.

I think that if modern novels are to be read at all, they should be taken like this, at one gulp, and then thrown away—preferably into the fire. . . .

Letter to Arthur Greeves, June 28, 1916 (*CL* 1)

MODERNISM IN LITERATURE AND ART

Many modern novels, poems, and pictures, which we are browbeaten into "appreciating," are not good work because they are not *work* at all. They are mere puddles of spilled sensibility or reflection. When an artist is in the strict sense working, he of course takes into account the existing taste, interests, and capacity of his audience. These, no less than the language, the marble, or the paint, are part of his raw material; to be used, tamed, sublimated, not ignored nor defied. Haughty indifference to them is not genius nor integrity; it is laziness and incompetence.

"Good Work and Good Works," *The World's Last Night*

MODERNISM AS THE WHINING AND MUMBLING PERIOD

Can it be—dare we hope—that the ghastly mumbling and whining period in which you and I have lived nearly all our lives, is really coming to an end? Shall we see gold and scarlet and flutes and trumpets come back?

Letter to Daphne Harwood, February 20, 1950 (*CL* 3)

SIR THOMAS MORE

Great claims have in modern times been made for More's English prose; I can accept them only with serious reservations. . . . The man who sits down and reads fairly through fifty pages of More will find many phrases to admire; but he will also find an invertebrate length of sentence, a fumbling multiplication of epithets, and an almost complete lack of rhythmical vitality. . . . Its chief cause is the fact that More never really rose from a legal to a literary conception of clarity and completeness. He multiplies words in a vain endeavor to stop up all possible chinks, where a better artist forces his conceptions on us by the light and heat of intellect and emotion in which they burn. He thus loses the advantages both of full writing and of concise writing. There are no lightning thrusts: and, on the other hand, no swelling tide of thought and feeling. The style is stodgy and doughlike. As for the good phrases, the reader will already have divined their nature. They come when More is in his homeliest vein: their race and pith and mere Englishry are the great redeeming feature of his prose. . . . Nearly all that is best in More is comic or close to comedy.

English Literature in the Sixteenth Century (Excluding Drama)

WHY LEWIS PREFERRED GEORGE ORWELL'S *ANIMAL FARM* TO *1984*

"*Animal Farm* is formally almost perfect; light, strong, balanced. There is not a sentence that does not contribute to the whole. The myth says all the author wants it to say and (equally important) it doesn't say anything else. Here is an *objet d'art* as durably satisfying as a Horatian ode or a Chippendale chair."

Here we have two books by the same author which deal, at bottom, with the same subject. Both are very bitter, honest, and honorable recantations. They express the disillusionment of one who had been a revolutionary of the familiar, *entre guerre* pattern and had later come to see that all totalitarian rulers, however their shirts may be colored, are equally the enemies of man.

Since the subject concerns us all and the disillusionment has been widely shared, it is not surprising that either book, or both, should find plenty of readers, and both are obviously the works of a very considerable writer. What puzzles me is the marked preference of the public for *1984*. For it seems to me (apart from its magnificent, and fortunately detachable, appendix on Newspeak) to be merely a flawed, interesting book; but the *Farm* is a work of genius which may well outlive the particular and (let us hope) temporary conditions that provoked it.

To begin with, it is very much the shorter of the two. This in itself would not, of course, show it to be the better. I am the last person to think so. Callimachus, to be sure, thought a great book a great evil, but then I think Callimachus a great prig. My appetite is hearty and when I sit down to read I like a square meal. But in this instance the shorter book seems to do all that the longer one does, and more. The longer book does not justify its greater length. There is dead wood in it. And I think we can all see where the dead wood comes.

In the nightmare state of *1984* the rulers devote a great deal of time—which means that the author and readers also have to devote a great deal of time—to a curious kind of anti-sexual propaganda. Indeed the amours of the hero and heroine seem to be at least as much a gesture of protest against that propaganda as a natural outcome of affection or appetite. . . .

But this is only the clearest instance of the defect which, throughout, makes *1984* inferior to the *Farm*. There is too much in it of the author's own psychology: too much indulgence of what he feels as a man, not pruned or mastered by what he intends to make as an artist. The *Farm* is work of a wholly different order.

Here the whole thing is projected and distanced. It becomes a myth and is allowed to speak for itself. The author shows us hateful things; he doesn't stammer or speak thick under the surge of his own hatred. The emotion no longer disables him because it has all been used, and used to make something.

One result is that the satire becomes more effective. Wit and humor (absent from the longer work) are employed with devastating effect. The great sentence "All animals are equal but some are more equal than others" bites deeper than the whole of *1984*.

Thus the shorter book does all that the longer does. But it also does more. Paradoxically, when Orwell turns all his characters into animals he makes them more fully human. In *1984* the cruelty of the tyrants is odious, but it is not tragic; odious like a man skinning a cat alive, not tragic like the cruelty of Regan and Goneril to Lear.

Tragedy demands a certain minimum stature in the victim; and the hero and heroine of *1984* do not reach that minimum. They become interesting at all only in so far as they suffer. That is claim enough (Heaven knows) on our sympathies in real life, but not in fiction. A central character who escapes nullity only by being tortured is a failure. And the hero and heroine in this story are surely such dull, mean little creatures that one might be introduced to them once a week for six months without even remembering them.

In *Animal Farm* all this is changed. The greed and cunning of the pigs is tragic (not merely odious) because we are made to care about all the honest, well-meaning, or even heroic beasts whom they exploit. The death of Boxer the horse moves us more than all the more elaborate cruelties of the other book. And not only moves, but convinces. Here, despite the animal disguise, we feel we are in a real world. This—this congeries of guzzling pigs, snapping dogs, and heroic horses—this is what humanity is like; very good, very bad, very pitiable, very honorable. If men were only like the people in *1984* it would hardly be worthwhile writing stories about them. It is as if Orwell could not see them until he put them into a beast fable.

Finally, *Animal Farm* is formally almost perfect; light, strong, balanced. There is not a sentence that does not contribute to the whole. The myth says all the author wants it to say and (equally important) it doesn't say anything else. Here is an *objet d'art* as durably satisfying as a Horatian ode or a Chippendale chair.

That is why I find the superior popularity of *1984* so discouraging. Something must, of course, be allowed for mere length. The booksellers say that short books will not sell. And there are reasons not discreditable. The weekend reader wants something that will last till Sunday evening; the traveler wants something that will last as far as Glasgow.

Again, *1984* belongs to a genre that is now more familiar than a beast fable; I mean the genre of what may be called dystopias, those nightmare visions of the future which began, perhaps, with Wells's *Time*

Machine and *The Sleeper Awakes*. I would like to hope that these causes are sufficient. Certainly, it would be alarming if we had to conclude either that the use of the imagination had so decayed that readers demand in all fiction a realistic surface and cannot treat any fable as more than a "juvenile," or else that the bed scenes in *1984* are the flavoring without which no book can now be sold.

"George Orwell," *On Stories*

BEATRIX POTTER

I only wish I could come and see you, especially if it included the chance of meeting Miss Potter. It was the professor of Anglo-Saxon [J. R. R. Tolkien] who first pointed out to me that her art of putting about ten words on one page so as to have a perfect rhythm and to answer just the questions a child would ask, is almost as severe as that of lyric poetry. She has a secure place among the masters of English prose.

Letter to Delmar Banner, November 30, 1942 (*CL* 2)

TO DOROTHY L. SAYERS ON HER TRANSLATION OF DANTE

One thing (though it now hinders me from writing as precisely about the work as I should like) will, I believe, please you—and Dante too. I set out with the intention of judging it as a translation: but in a few cantos I'd forgotten all about that and was thinking only of Dante. And then, a few cantos later, I forgot all about Dante and thought only about purgatory. In a word, the double mechanism worked and therefore made no noise. It is a novel form of praise to say, when asked about your share in the performance, "I didn't *notice* it." But I think it's perhaps the highest one can give a translation. *Bene olet ubi nihil olet.* [(A woman) smells right when nothing smells.]

Letter to Dorothy L. Sayers, July 31, 1955 (*CL* 3)

THE CIVILIZED HEART IN SCOTT, DICKENS, AND TOLSTOY

I *have* a taste for Dickens but don't think it a low one. He is the great author on mere *affection*: only he and Tolstoy (another great favorite of mine) really deal with it. Of course his error lies in thinking it will do instead of agape [self-giving, godlike love]. Scott, as D. Cecil said, has not the civilized *mind*, but the civilized *heart*. Unforced nobility, generosity, liberality, flow from him.

Letter to Dom Bede Griffiths, January 23, 1954 (*CL* 3)

TWO SPECIES OF EXCELLENCE IN WILLIAM SHAKESPEARE

The mark of Shakespeare (and it is quite enough for one mortal man) is simply this: to have combined two species of excellence which are not, in a remarkable degree, combined by any other artist, namely the imaginative splendor of the highest type of lyric and the realistic presentation of human life and character.

"Variation in Shakespeare and Others," *Selected Literary Essays*

SHAKESPEARE'S *HAMLET* AS A FAILURE BETTER THAN SUCCESS

"Most certainly an artistic failure."[4] All argument is for that conclusion——until you read or see *Hamlet* again. And when you do, you are left saying that if this is failure, then failure is better than success. We

---

4 T. S. Eliot's assessment of the play

want more of these "bad" plays. From our first childish reading of the ghost scenes down to those golden
minutes which we stole from marking examination
papers on *Hamlet* to read a few pages of *Hamlet* itself, have we ever known the day or the hour when
its enchantment failed? . . . It has a taste of its own,
an all-pervading relish which we recognize even in its
smallest fragments, and which, once tasted, we recur
to. When we want that taste, no other book will do
instead.

"Hamlet: The Prince or the Poem?," *Selected Literary Essays*

SHAKESPEARE ON THE LASTING MYSTERY OF THE HUMAN SITUATION

I believe that we read Hamlet's speeches with interest
chiefly because they describe so well a certain spiritual
region through which most of us have passed and anyone in his circumstances might be expected to pass. . . .

The real and lasting mystery of our human situation has been greatly depicted.

"Hamlet: The Prince or the Poem?," *Selected Literary Essays*

PERCY SHELLEY'S *PROMETHEUS UNBOUND*

The resulting whole [*Prometheus Unbound*] is the greatest long poem in the nineteenth century, and the only long poem of the highest kind in that century which approaches to perfection. . . .

For my own part I believe that no poet has felt more keenly, or presented more weightily the necessity for a complete unmaking and remaking of man, to be endured at the dark bases of his being. I do not know the book (in profane literature) to which I should turn for a like expression of what von Hügel would have called the "costingness" of regeneration. . . .

The fourth act I shall not attempt to analyze. It is

an intoxication, a riot, a complicated and uncontrollable splendor, long, and yet not too long, sustained on the note of ecstasy such as no other English poet, perhaps no other poet, has given us. It can be achieved by more than one artist in music: to do it in words has been, I think, beyond the reach of nearly all.

"Shelley, Dryden, and Mr. Eliot," *Selected Literary Essays*

PHILIP SIDNEY'S *ARCADIA*

I have just had the pleasure of reading Sidney's *Arcadia*. . . . The book itself is a glorious feast: I don't know how to explain its particular charm, because it is not at all like anything I ever read before: and yet in places like all of them. Sometimes it is like Malory, often like Spenser, and yet different from either. For one thing, there is a fine description of scenery in it (only one so far, but I hope for more) which neither of them could have done. Then again the figure of the shepherd boy "piping as though he would never be old" rather reminds me of *The Crock of Gold* [by James Stephens, 1912]. But all this comes to is that Sidney is not like anyone else, but is just himself.

Letter to Arthur Greeves, June 20, 1916 (*CL* 1)

EDMUND SPENSER'S *THE FAERIE QUEENE*

From the time of its publication down to about 1914 it was everyone's poem—the book in which many and many a boy first discovered that he liked poetry; a book which spoke at once, like Homer or Shakespeare or Dickens, to every reader's imagination. Spenser did not rank as a hard poet like Pindar, Donne, or Browning. How we have lost that approach I do not know. And unfortunately *The Faerie Queene* suffers even more than most great works from being approached through the medium of commentaries and "literary history." . . . The poem is a great palace, but the door into it is so low that you must stoop to go in. No prig can be a Spenserian. It is of course much more than a fairy tale, but unless we can enjoy it as a fairy tale first of all, we shall not really care for it.

"Edmund Spenser," *Studies in Medieval and Renaissance Literature*

LAURENCE STERNE'S *TRISTRAM SHANDY*

I have read today . . . some ten pages of *Tristram Shandy* and am wondering whether I like it. It is certainly the maddest book ever written. . . . It gives you the impression of an escaped lunatic's conversation while chasing his hat on a windy May morning.

Letter to Arthur Greeves, October 25, 1916 (*CL* 1)

WILLIAM MAKEPEACE THACKERAY

The trouble with Thackeray is that he can hardly envisage goodness except as a kind of good-heartedness: all his "good" people are not only simple, but simpletons. That is a subtle poison which comes in with the Renaissance: the Machiavellian (intelligent) villain presently producing the idiot hero. The Middle Ages didn't make Herod clever and knew the devil was an ass. There is really an unfaith about Thackeray's ethics: as if goodness were somehow charming and "seelie" [silly] and infantile. No conception that the purification of the will (ceteris paribus [other things being equal]) leads to the enlightenment of the intelligence.

Letter to Dom Bede Griffiths, January 30, 1954 (*CL* 3)

LEWIS'S REVIEW OF J. R. R. TOLKIEN'S
THE HOBBIT

"To define the world of *The Hobbit* is, of course, impossible, because it is new. You cannot anticipate it before you go there, as you cannot forget it once you have gone."

The publishers claim that *The Hobbit*, though very unlike *Alice*, resembles it in being the work of a professor at play. A more important truth is that both belong to a very small class of books which have nothing in common save that each admits us to a world of its own—a world that seems to have been going on before we stumbled into it but which, once found by the right reader, becomes indispensable to him. Its place is with *Alice, Flatland, Phantastes, The Wind in the Willows*.

To define the world of *The Hobbit* is, of course, impossible, because it is new. You cannot anticipate it

C. S. LEWIS

before you go there, as you cannot forget it once you have gone. . . .

You must read for yourself to find out how inevitable the change is and how it keeps pace with the hero's journey. Though all is marvelous, nothing is arbitrary: all the inhabitants of Wilderland seem to have the same unquestionable right to their existence as those of our own world, though the fortunate child who meets them will have no notion—and his unlearned elders not much more—of the deep sources in our blood and tradition from which they spring.

For it must be understood that this is a children's book only in the sense that the first of many readings can be undertaken in the nursery. *Alice* is read gravely by children and with laughter by grown-ups; *The Hobbit*, on the other hand, will be funniest to its youngest readers, and only years later, at a tenth or a twentieth reading, will they begin to realize what deft scholarship and profound reflection have gone to make everything in it so ripe, so friendly, and in its own way so true. Prediction is dangerous: but *The Hobbit* may well prove a classic.

"The Hobbit," *On Stories and Other Essays on Literature*

LEWIS'S REVIEW OF J. R. R. TOLKIEN'S *THE LORD OF THE RINGS*

This book is like lightning from a clear sky; as sharply different, as unpredictable in our age as *Songs of Innocence* were in theirs. To say that in it heroic romance, gorgeous, eloquent, and unashamed, has suddenly returned at a period almost pathological in its anti-romanticism is inadequate. To us, who live in that odd period, the return—and the sheer relief of it—is doubtless the important thing. But in the history of romance itself—a history which stretches back to *The Odyssey* and beyond—it makes not a return but an advance or revolution: the conquest of new territory.

Nothing quite like it was ever done before. "One takes it," says Naomi Mitchison, "as seriously as Malory." But then the ineluctable sense of reality which we feel in *Le Morte d'Arthur* comes largely from the great weight of other men's work built up century by century, which has gone into it. The utterly new achievement of Professor Tolkien is that he carries a comparable sense of reality unaided. Probably no book yet written in the world is quite such a radical instance of what its author has ere called "subcreation." The direct debt (there are of course subtler kinds of debt) which every author must owe to the actual universe is here deliberately reduced to the minimum. Not content to create his own story, he creates, with an almost insolent prodigality, the whole world in which it is to move, with its own theology, myths, geography, history, paleography, languages, and orders of beings—a world "full of strange creatures beyond count." The names alone are a feast, whether redolent of quiet countryside (Michel Delving, Southfarthing), tall and kingly (Boromir, Faramir, Elendil), loathsome like Sméagol, who is also Gollum, or frowning in the evil strength of Barad-dûr or Gorgoroth; yet best of all (Lothlórien, Gilthoniel, Galadriel) when they embody that piercing, high elvish beauty of which no other prose writer has captured so much.

Such a book has of course its predestined readers, even now more numerous and more critical than is always realized. To them a reviewer need say little, except that here are beauties which pierce like swords or burn like cold iron; here is a book that will break your heart. They will know that this is good news, good beyond hope. To complete their happiness one need only add that it promises to be gloriously long: this volume is only the first of three. But it is too great a book to rule only its natural subjects. Something must be said to "those without," to the unconverted. At the very least, possible misunderstandings may be got out of the way.

First, we must clearly understand that though *The*

Fellowship in one way continues its author's fairy tale, *The Hobbit,* it is in no sense an overgrown "juvenile." The truth is the other way round. *The Hobbit* was merely a fragment torn from the author's huge myth and adapted for children; inevitably losing something by the adaptation. *The Fellowship* gives us at last the lineaments of that myth "in their true dimensions like themselves." Misunderstanding on this point might easily be encouraged by the first chapter, in which the author (taking a risk) writes almost in the manner of the earlier and far lighter book. With some who will find the main body of the book deeply moving, this chapter may not be a favorite.

Yet there were good reasons for such an opening; still more for the prologue (wholly admirable, this) which precedes it. It is essential that we should first be well steeped in the "homeliness," the frivolity, even (in its best sense) the vulgarity of the creatures called Hobbits; these unambitious folk, peaceable yet almost anarchical, with faces "good-natured rather than beautiful" and "mouths apt to laughter and eating," who treat smoking as an art and like books which tell them what they already know. They are not an allegory of the English, but they are perhaps a myth that only an Englishman (or, should we add, a Dutchman?) could have created. Almost the central theme of the book is the contrast between the Hobbits (or "the Shire") and the appalling destiny to which some of them are called, the terrifying discovery that the humdrum happiness of the Shire, which they had taken for granted as something normal, is in reality a sort of local and temporary accident, that its existence depends on being protected by powers which Hobbits dare not imagine, that any Hobbit may find himself forced out of the Shire and caught up into that high conflict. More strangely still, the event of that conflict between strongest things may come to depend on him, who is almost the weakest.

What shows that we are reading myth, not allegory, is that there are no pointers to a specifically theological, or political, or psychological application. A myth points, for each reader, to the realm he lives in most. It is a master key; use it on what door you like. And there are other themes in *The Fellowship* equally serious.

That is why no catchwords about "escapism" or "nostalgia" and no distrust of "private worlds" are in court. This is no Angria, no dreaming; it is sane and vigilant invention, revealing at point after point the integration of the author's mind. What is the use of calling "private" a world we can all walk into and test and in which we find such a balance? As for escapism, what we chiefly escape is the illusions of our ordinary life. We certainly do not escape anguish. Despite many a snug fireside and many an hour of good cheer to gratify the hobbit in each of us, anguish is, for me, almost the prevailing note. But not, as in the literature most typical of our age, the anguish of abnormal or contorted souls: rather that anguish of those who were happy before a certain darkness came up and will be happy if they live to see it gone.

Nostalgia does indeed come in; not ours nor the author's, but that of the characters. . . . Our own world, except at certain rare moments, hardly seems so heavy with its past. This is one element in the anguish which the characters bear. But with the anguish there comes also a strange exaltation. They are at once stricken and upheld by the memory of vanished civilizations and lost splendor. They have outlived the second and third ages; the wine of life was drawn long since. As we read we find ourselves sharing their burden; when we have finished, we return to our own life not relaxed but fortified.

But there is more in the book still. Every now and then, risen from sources we can only conjecture and almost alien (one would think) to the author's habitual imagination, figures meet us so brimming with life (not human life) that they make our sort of anguish and our sort of exaltation seem unimportant. Such is Tom Bombadil, such the unforgettable Ents. This is surely the utmost reach of invention, when an author produces what seems to be not even his own, much less anyone else's. Is mythopoeia, after all, not the most, but the least, subjective of activities?

Even now I have left out almost everything—the sylvan leafiness, the passions, the high virtues, the remote horizons. Even if I had space, I could hardly convey them. And after all the most obvious appeal of the book is perhaps also its deepest: "There was sorrow then too, and gathering dark, but great valor, and great deeds that were not wholly vain." *Not wholly vain*—it is the cool middle point between illusion and disillusionment.

When I reviewed the first volume of this work I hardly dared to hope it would have the success which I was sure it deserved. Happily I am proved wrong. There is, however, one piece of false criticism which had better be answered: the complaint that the characters are all either black or white. Since the climax of Volume 1 was mainly concerned with the struggle between good and evil in the mind of Boromir, it is not easy to see how anyone could have said this. I will hazard a guess. "How shall a man judge what to do in such times?" asks someone in Volume 2. "As he has ever judged," comes the reply. "Good and ill have not changed . . . nor are they one thing among Elves and Dwarves and another among Men."

This is the basis of the whole Tolkienian world. I think some readers, seeing (and disliking) this rigid demarcation of black and white, imagine they have seen a rigid demarcation between black and white people. Looking at the squares, they assume (in defiance of the facts) that all the pieces must be making bishops' moves which confine them to one color. But even such readers will hardly brazen it out through the two last volumes. Motives, even in the right side, are mixed. Those who are now traitors usually began with comparatively innocent intentions. Heroic Rohan and imperial Gondor are partly diseased. Even the wretched Sméagol, till quite late in the story, has good impulses; and (by a tragic paradox) what finally pushes him over the brink is an unpremeditated speech by the most selfless character of all. . . .

Of picking out great moments (such as the cockcrow at the Siege of Gondor) there would be no end; I will mention two general (and totally different) excellences. One, surprisingly, is realisms. This war has the very quality of the war my generation knew. It is all here: the endless, unintelligible movement, the sinister quiet of the front when "everything is now ready," the flying civilians, the lively, vivid friendships, the background of something like despair and the merry foreground, and such heaven-sent windfalls as a *cache* of choice to-bacco "salvaged" from a ruin. The author has told us elsewhere that his taste for fairy tale was wakened into maturity by active service; that, no doubt, is why we can say of his war scenes (quoting Gimli the Dwarf), "There is good rock here. This country has tough bones." The other excellence is that no individual, and no species, seems to exist only for the sake of the plot. All exist in their own right and would have been worth creating for their mere flavor even if they had been irrelevant. Treebeard would have served any other author (if any other could have conceived him) for a whole book. His eyes are "filled up with ages of memory and long, slow, steady thinking." Through those ages his name has grown with him, so that he cannot now tell it; it would, by now, take too long to pronounce. When he learns that the thing they are standing on is a hill, he complains that this is but "a hasty word" for that which has so much history in it.

How far Treebeard can be regarded as a "portrait of the artist" must remain doubtful; but when he hears that some people want to identify the Ring with the hydrogen bomb, and Mordor with Russia, I think he might call it a "hasty" word. How long do people think a world like his takes to grow? Do they think it can be done as quickly as a modern nation changes its public enemy number one or as modern scientists invent new weapons? When Professor Tolkien began there was probably no nuclear fission and the contemporary incarnation of Mordor was a good deal nearer our shores. But the text itself teaches us that Sauron is eternal; the war of the Ring is only one of a thousand wars against him. Every time we shall be wise to fear his ultimate victory, after which there will be "no more songs." Again and again we shall have good evidence that "the wind is setting East, and the withering of all woods may be drawing near." Every time we win we shall know that our victory is impermanent. If we insist on asking for the moral of the story, that is its moral: a recall from facile optimism and wailing pessimism alike, to that hard, yet not quite desperate, insight into man's unchanging predicament by which heroic ages have lived. It is here that the Norse affinity is strongest: hammer strokes, but with compassion.

"But why," (some ask), "why, if you have a serious comment to make on the real life of men, must you do it by talking about a phantasmagoric never-never land of your own?" Because, I take it, one of the main things the author wants to say is that the real life of men is of that mythical and heroic quality. One can see the principle at work in his characterization. Much that in a realistic work would be done by "character delineation" is here done simply by making the character an elf, a dwarf, or a hobbit. The imagined beings have their insides on the outside; they are visible souls. And man as a whole, man pitted against the universe, have we seen him at all till we see that he is like a hero in a fairy tale? In the book Éomer rashly contrasts "the green earth" with "legends." Aragorn replies that the green earth itself is "a mighty matter of legend."

The value of the myth is that it takes all the things we know and restores to them the rich significance which has been hidden by "the veil of familiarity." The child enjoys his cold meat (otherwise dull to him) by pretending it is buffalo, just killed with his own bow and arrow. And the child is wise. The real meat comes back to him more savory for having been dipped in a story; you might say that only then is it the real meat. If you are tired of the real landscape, look at it in a mirror. By putting bread, gold, horse, apple, or the very roads into a myth, we do not retreat from reality: we rediscover it. As long as the story lingers in our mind, the real things are more themselves. This book applies the treatment not only to bread or apple but to good and evil, to our endless perils, our anguish, and our joys. By dipping them in myth we see them more clearly. I do not think he could have done it in any other way.

The book is too original and too opulent for any final judgment on a first reading. But we know at once that it has done things to us. We are not quite the same men. And though we must ration ourselves in our rereadings, I have little doubt that the book will soon take its place among the indispensables.

"Tolkien's *The Lord of the Rings*," *On Stories*

LEO TOLSTOY

The most interesting thing that has happened to me since I last wrote is reading *War and Peace*—at least I am now in the middle of the fourth and last volume so I think, bar accidents, I am pretty sure to finish it. It has completely changed my view of novels.

Hitherto I had always looked on them as rather a *dangerous* form—I mean dangerous to the health of literature as a whole. I thought that the strong "narrative lust"—the passionate itch to "see what happened in the end"—which novels aroused, necessarily injured the taste for other, better, but less irresistible, forms of literary pleasure: and that the growth of novel reading largely explained the deplorable division of readers into low-brow and high-brow—the low being simply those who had learned to expect from books this "narrative lust" from the time they began to read, and who had thus destroyed in advance their possible taste for better things. I also thought that the intense desire which novels rouse in us for the "happiness" of the chief characters (no one feels that way about Hamlet or Othello) and the selfishness with which this happiness is concerned, were thoroughly bad. . . .

Tolstoy, in this book, has changed all that. I have felt everywhere, in a sense—you will know what I mean—that sublime *indifference* to the life or death, success or failure, of the chief characters, which is not a *blank* indifference at all, but almost like submission to the will of God. Then the variety of it. The war parts are just the best descriptions of war ever written: all the modern war books are milk and water to this: then the rural parts—lovely pictures of village life and of religious festivals in which the relations between the peasants and the nobles almost make you forgive feudalism; the society parts, in which I was astonished to find so much humor—there is a great hostess who always separates two guests when she sees them getting really interested in conversation, who is almost a Jane Austen character. There are love passages that have the same sort of intoxicating quality you get in Meredith—and passages about soldiers chatting over fires which remind one of Patsy Macan, and a drive in a sledge by moonlight which is better than Hans Andersen.

Letter to Arthur Greeves, March 29, 1931 (*CL* 1)

THOMAS TRAHERNE'S *CENTURIES OF MEDITATIONS*

At present I'm rereading [Thomas] Traherne's *Centuries of Meditations*, which I think almost the most beautiful book (in prose, I mean, excluding poets) in English.

Letter to Arthur Greeves, December 23, 1941 (*CL* 2)

H. G. WELLS'S *MARRIAGE*

You will be surprised when you hear how I employed the return journey—by reading an H. G. Wells novel called *Marriage* [1912], and perhaps more surprised when I say that I thoroughly enjoyed it; one thing you can say for the man is that he really is interested in all the big, outside questions—and the characters are intensely real, especially a Mr. Pope who reminds me of Excellenz [Lewis's father]. It opens new landscapes to me—how one felt that on finding that a new kind of book was waiting for one, in the old days—and I have decided to read some more of his serious books. It is funny that I—and perhaps you—read the old books for pleasure and always turn to contemporaries with the notion of "improving my mind." With most, I fancy, the direct opposite is so.

Letter to Arthur Greeves, February 3, 1920 (*CL* 1)

T. H. WHITE'S *THE SWORD IN THE STONE*

The Sword in the Stone [is] one of the most deeply vulgar books I've ever read. Its humor is exactly on the level of an urchin with a lead pencil drawing a mustache on the lip of a classical statue. . . . It is the work of a sad, shabby little mind.

Letter to George Every, December 11, 1940 (*CL* 2)

WALT WHITMAN

The poetic species to which they belong—which might be called the rhapsodical—is one to which I am very insensitive: I can't bear Walt Whitman.

My feeling is that the more vast and supersensible a poem's subject is, the more it needs to be fixed, founded, incarnated in regular meter and concrete images.

Letter to Robert Longacre, June 19, 1952 (*CL* 3)

NOTE TO CHARLES WILLIAMS ON HIS NOVEL
DESCENT INTO HELL

I hope this doesn't sound patronizing—in sheer writing I think you have gone up, as we examiners say, a whole class. Chapter 2 is in my opinion your high-water mark so far. You have completely overcome a certain flamboyance which I always thought your chief danger: this is crisp as grape nuts, hard as a hammer, clear as glass. I am a little worried in the Wentworth part by the tendency to Gertrude Steinisms[5] ("eaves"/"eves," "guard"/"card," etc.).

Letter to Charles Williams, September 23, 1937 (*CL* 2)

---

5 An early twentieth-century American poet disliked by many British poets of the time

BIBLIOGRAPHY

» *The Allegory of Love: A Study in Medieval Tradition*. Oxford: Oxford University Press, 1936.

» *Christian Reflections*. Grand Rapids, MI: Wm. B. Eerdmans Publishing Co., 1967.

» *The Collected Letters of C. S. Lewis* Volume 1, *Family Letters, 1905–1931*, edited by Walter Hooper. San Francisco: HarperOne, 2000.

» *The Collected Letters of C. S. Lewis* Volume 2, *Books, Broadcasts, and the War, 1931–1949*, edited by Walter Hooper. San Francisco: HarperOne, 2004.

» *The Collected Letters of C. S. Lewis* Volume 3, *Narnia, Cambridge, and Joy, 1950–1963*, edited by Walter Hooper. San Francisco: HarperOne, 2007.

» *English Literature in the Sixteenth Century (Excluding Drama)*. New York: HarperOne. Reissued 2022.

» *God in the Dock*. Edited by Walter Hooper. Grand Rapids, MI: William B. Eerdmans Publishing Company, 1970.

» *Of Other Worlds: Essays and Stories*. New York: HarperOne. Reissued 2017.

» *On Stories and Other Essays on Literature*. New York: HarperOne. Reissued 2017.

» *Reflections on the Psalms*. New York: HarperOne. Reissued 2017.

BIBLIOGRAPHY

» *Selected Literary Essays*. Edited by Walter Hooper. Cambridge: Cambridge University Press, 1969.

» *Spenser's Images of Life*. Cambridge: Cambridge University Press. Reissued 2013.

» *Studies in Medieval and Renaissance Literature*. Cambridge: Cambridge University Press, 1966, 1998, 2013.

» *Studies in Words*. 2nd edition. Cambridge: Cambridge University Press, 1960, 1967, 2013.

» *The Weight of Glory and Other Addresses*. Grand Rapids, MI: William B. Eerdmans Publishing Co., 1949.

» *The World's Last Night and Other Essays*. New York: HarperOne. Reissued 2013.